Lead Great Virtual Meetings

The Steps You Need to Succeed

Bernice L. Ross, Ph.D.
and
Byron Van Arsdale

Published in the United States of America by
Rossdale Press
a subsidiary of BrokerageUP, Inc.
12400 Highway 71 West
Suite 350, PMB 343
Austin, Texas 78738

Ross, Bernice L.
Van Arsdale, Byron
Lead Great Virtual Meetings:
The Steps You Need to Succeed

ISBN: 978-0-9985573-2-8

Copyright © 2021
by Bernice L. Ross and Byron Van Arsdale
All rights reserved in all media.

Cover Design by F + P Graphic Design

No part of this book may be reproduced, stored in a retrieval system, or transmitted by any means, electronic, mechanical, photocopying, recording, or othewise, without written permission from the author.

This book contains information of a general nature. As laws may vary from state to state, readers should consult a competent professional regarding their own particular state laws. The business world is ever changing and dynamic and involves risks and uncertainties. The authors and publisher cannot and do not warrant or guarantee that use of information in this book will work for you.

To Shane Bowlin:

You are the wind beneath our wings

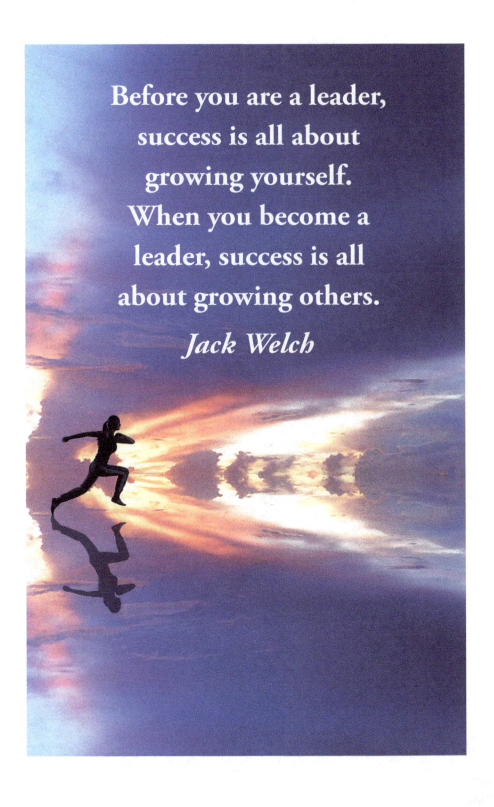

Table of Contents

Chapter 1: The Virtual Meeting Revolution — 13
What is a Virtual Meeting?
Over 100 Years of Virtual Meetings
My Journey with the Virtual Meeting Model
The Birth of The Six Principle Model
What Makes an Effective Virtual Meeting Leader?
Chapter 1 Key Points

Chapter 2: The Six Principle Model — 19
The Six Principles
Principle #1: People Listen for Their Reasons, Not Yours
Principle #2: People Support What They Help to Create
Principle #3: Connection, Connection, Connection
Principle #4: Surface the Wisdom of the Group
Case Study
Principle #5: Flex Your Flexibility Muscle
Principle #6: What You Do is What You Get
Additional Fundamentals You Need to Know
Applying The Six Principle Model
Chapter 2 Key Points

Chapter 3: Challenges Leading in an All Auditory Environment — 37
We're Wired to Be Visual
Generational Differences
Monday Morning Blues: The Anatomy of a Poorly Led Conference Call
Chapter 3 Key Points

Chapter 4: Technology Basics — 45
Pre-Meeting Technology Checklist
Hiss, Pop, Buzz, Snore: Minimizing Annoying Distractions During Auditory Meetings
Chapter 4 Key Points

Chapter 5: Best Practices that Work Across Multiple Delivery Platforms   53
    Twelve Guidelines to Follow on Every Virtual Meeting
    Chapter 5 Key Points

Chapter 6: Issues to Address Before Your Video-Based Virtual Meeting   63
    Different Platforms, Different Strategies
    Six Primary Methods for Delivering Content
    What Tools and Systems Will You Need?
    Tech Decisions You Must Address
    Logistics
    Content Decisions
    Fifteen Best Practices to Follow as You Plan Your Meeting
    Case Study: Using Polling to Ramp Up Interactivity
    Chapter 6 Key Points

Chapter 7: How to Create a High Impact Presentation   79
    Four Major Types of Virtual Meetings
    What's the Purpose of Your Meeting?
    Are You a Deductive or Inductive Content Creator?
    Slide Construction 101: How to Engage Your Viewers
    Twenty Ways to Make Your Slide Deck More Engaging
    Chapter 7 Key Points

Chapter 8: Improve Your Delivery   103
    Interactive Video or Webinar?
    Start Strong and End Strong
    How Fast Do You Speak?
    Visual, Auditory, or Kinesthetic—How Is Your Brain Wired?
    Use Your Voice to Manage the Room
    Avoid the Following Words that Weaken Your Delivery
    Control Your Body Language

Record Yourself
Chapter 8 Key Points

Chapter 9: Meeting Day: Fifteen Common Mistakes to Avoid — 115

    Common Mistake #1: Failure to Systematize How You Handle Logistics
    Common Mistake #2: Failure to Review Your Slide Deck the Evening Before and the Day of Your Meeting
    Common Mistake #3: Failure to Send Out "Guidelines for Participants"
    Common Mistake #4: Arriving Less Than 30 Minutes Before the Start Time
    Common Mistake #5: "Waiting for Organizer"
    Common Mistake #6: Not Attending to the Housekeeping First
    Common Mistake #7: Not Providing Your Supporting Materials Prior to the Meeting
    Common Mistake #8: Long Intros
    Common Mistake #9: Not Telling Them What You're Going to Tell Them
    Common Mistake #10: The "Content Download"
    Common Mistake #11: Believing You Cannot Create Interactivity During Asynchronous Meetings and Classes
    Common Mistake #12: It's All About Me!
    Common Mistake #13: Reading the Slides to Your Participants
    Common Mistake #14: Packing Too Much Content on a Single Slide
    Common Mistake #15: Not Ending on Time
    Chapter 9 Key Points

Chapter 10: Zoom Your Way to Success   129
From the Boardroom to the Bedroom
Why Video-Based Virtual Meetings Make Leaders
    So Uncomfortable
The Basics
Real or Virtual Background?
How to Create a "Zoom Room"
Thirty Seconds of Challenges
Analyzing What Went Wrong
How to Avoid "Zoom Fatigue"
Four Real Estate Case Studies: How to Put Zoom to
    Work in Your Organization
Case Study #1 Texas Realtors: How We Delivered
    Live CE Training to 500 Locations Simultaneously
Using Zoom
Case Study #2 *The Wall Street Journal (WSJ)*:
    Zoom Town halls and Conventions
Case Study #3 EXIT Realty: Leverage Your Zoom
    Meetings to Provide Better Service and Build
    Relationships
Case Study #4 Fidelity National Title Agency: Connect
    and Have Fun
Make Your Backgrounds Ultra-Personal
Chapter 10 Key Points

Chapter 11: Leading in the Dark   155
The Monologue Challenge: Building Engagement During
    Asynchronous Meetings
Vary Your Visuals to Keep Participants Engaged
Learning Management Systems (LMS)
Case Study
Avatar-Based-Platforms
Chapter 11 Key Points

Chapter 12: Which Principles and Tools Will You Use as You Lead?   189
    Two Simple Steps to Take Before Your Next Virtual Meeting
    Stay Focused on Your Participants: Use "You," Not "I" or "Me"
    Case Study: Twelve Real World Applications of The Six Principle Model
    Audio-Only Meetings
    Video Conferencing
    Where to Concentrate Your Focus
    How Will You Know When You Have Mastered The Six Principles?
    Chapter 12 Key Points

Acknowledgements   207

Appendix A: Guidelines for Participants   211

Appendix B: Guidelines for Creating a Talking Circle   213
    Talking Circle Guidelines for Your Participants
    Outcomes You Can Achieve Using the Talking Circle
    Using the Talking Circle as a Counseling Tool

About the Authors   219

Chapter 1:
The Virtual Meeting Revolution

*You cannot change your destination overnight,
but you can change your direction overnight.*
Jim Rohn

Have you ever been on a poorly run conference call, webinar, video conference, or other virtual meeting? What about attending a boring class that was a waste of your time? Rather than engaging, you were probably catching up on your email, text messaging, or staying up-to-date on Facebook and Instagram.

The 2020 COVID-19 pandemic plunged the world into relying on virtual communication as the primary means of connection. As business and personal communication shifted from face-to-face to being almost entirely virtual, millions faced the daunting task of learning how to use Zoom, Skype, or other online virtual meeting services.

Granted, there were plenty of tips, techniques, and best practices explaining how to use the various delivery platforms. Nevertheless, the most important element for leading virtual meetings and classes in this new environment was missing—a clear-cut leadership model addressing what is required to lead these types of meetings. Moreover, no one had addressed what it takes to be a good participant.

What is a Virtual Meeting?

For the purposes of this book, a virtual meeting links two or more people in two separate locations via electronic or digital means. It includes conference calls, teleclasses, video conferencing, webinars, classes delivered on Learning Management Systems (LMS), and on Avatar-Based-Platforms (ABPs). These may be synchronous (in real time) or asynchronous (recorded for replay).

Over 100 Years of Virtual Meetings

The first virtual meeting took place in 1915 when the first conference call was made to celebrate the Panama-Pacific International Exposition.

The cost was $485.00 per minute, the equivalent of over $12,340 per minute today!

Have you ever given any thought as to what is the most important aspect of your virtual meeting? The success or failure of EVERY virtual meeting is based upon what takes place in the auditory environment. No matter how sophisticated the technology is, the audio component is primary. When you lose the audio, your virtual meeting is over. Consequently, understanding the dynamics of how to lead effective virtual meetings begins and ends with the audio feed.

Although conference call technology is over 100 years old, the predominant approach today to leading ALL types of virtual meetings is still trial and error. There are two reasons leaders are stuck with this approach. First, while there are a wealth of technology tips and tactical strategies for leading conference calls and virtual meetings, most lack a cohesive virtual meeting leadership model. The second missing component is how to integrate the leader's unique leadership skills with the delivery platform the leader is using.

My Journey with the Virtual Meeting Model

My journey with the virtual meeting model began in late 1996. I was a Professor of Psychology at Los Angeles Pierce College while also serving as the Executive Director of Training for the 4,000 agent Jon Douglas Company. Lou Piatt, the president of the company, gave me a seemingly impossible task:

> *I want you to figure out a way to deliver training to all 60 of our offices. By the way, we don't have any budget.*

Fortunately, he did have an idea about to overcome this seemingly insurmountable problem.

> *I want you to investigate an organization called Coach University. They're doing all their training classes by phone.*

After our meeting, I checked out the CoachU website (coachu.com) and signed up for their four-week introductory coaching course. Their entire curriculum was based upon "teleclasses," i.e., interactive training conference calls with no more than 20 participants.

What intrigued me most, however, was their approach to coaching and how it aligned with cognitive behavioral psychology, my primary specialization during my doctoral studies. Instead of seeing the client as someone who needs to be fixed or helped as many therapists and untrained coaches do, CoachU founder Thomas Leonard viewed clients as being fully capable, fully resourceful, and fully functional. Coaching was about supporting the client to take the action steps that move them forward today, not on some past conflict or issue.

I enrolled in the CoachU certification program and began taking teleclasses. In February of 1997, I took a teleclass called "Challenging." Byron Van Arsdale was the leader. He had deep experience conducting leadership training for corporate, private, and public sector organizations. He was also an accomplished professional speaker.

I was extremely impressed with the level of trust, connection, and interactivity on his calls; it was unlike anything I had experienced before. What surprised me most was how a well-led teleclass was more personal, interactive, and effective than most face-to-face training I had attended. It was definitely something I wanted to explore.

After I completed the class requirements to qualify for the CoachU Teleclass Leader Training Program, I began my teleclass leader training with Byron. His background in real estate turned out to be an additional plus.

I went on to become an instructor at CoachU and employed many of Byron's strategies and techniques. I also began using the teleclass model at the Jon Douglas Company as well as with the senior administrative team at the Los Angeles Community College District where I was teaching.

The Birth of The Six Principle Model

In 1998, Byron formalized the very first leadership model for conference calls and teleclasses: The Six Principle Model. Because this model addresses who you are as a leader, how you will interact with those attending your meetings, plus how to handle the challenges you face leading in a virtual environment, it is the most important part of this book.

At first glance, The Six Principles may seem simplistic. Don't be deceived. The model is much like peeling an onion. The different layers become evident as you grow your skills. Furthermore, this model is more critical today than ever.

Since creating The Six Principle Model, Byron has trained over 2,000 professional business and personal coaches internationally using his model. The model has proven its effectiveness in virtual and face-to-face meetings with both public and private sector meetings including Coldwell Banker, IBM, Kaiser Permanente, the Los Angeles Community College District, Motorola, the State of Texas, the City of Austin, and numerous non-profits.

What Makes an Effective Virtual Meeting Leader?

Recall a favorite teacher, leader, or speaker who inspired you, or the boss who really got things done. What differentiated them from other individuals whose meetings or classes lacked inspiration and accomplished next to nothing?

The difference comes down to two words: connection and engagement. As I watched how Byron led teleclasses, three things stood out.

1. He seemed to quickly build connection on his calls, something most conference call and teleclass leaders struggle to do.

2. He regularly endorsed others and their contributions to the call.

3. There was a tremendous sense of safety and trust. This resulted in people being more open and forthcoming than I had ever seen in any other meeting environment

Byron helped me to understand what makes an effective virtual meeting leader is the same factor that makes someone an excellent coach—Leonard's notion the client is fully capable, fully resourceful, and fully functional.

Second, the sense of trust he created during his calls resulted from how he set up the "space." This powerful concept applies in both your professional and your personal life. To illustrate how this works, a classroom teacher holds the space for her students. She determines what happens in her classroom. Her students, however, are the ones who ultimately decide how they will act in her classroom and what they choose to learn once they leave it.

By the same token, parents "hold space" for their children. Parents are responsible for feeding them, clothing them, and providing them with shelter. Parents create the space known as "home," but what happens in that space is an interplay between all the people who live there, their pets, and all the other factors tied to the physical space as well.

The question every virtual meeting leader must answer is how to strengthen their connection with the people attending the meeting, regardless of the delivery mechanism or technology involved. Strong connection creates engagement, which in turn, creates the trust leading to great results. Poor connection and lack of engagement can result in frustration, resentment, and resistance.

No matter what type of virtual meeting you lead, you no longer need to rely on trial and error. *Lead Great Virtual Meetings* unlocks the secrets you need to shortcut the trial and error process and immediately begin working with the proven best practices, tips, and strategies we have discovered from working with The Six Principle Model.

By reading this book, you have already demonstrated your desire to improve your virtual leadership skills. We view you as being fully capable, fully resourceful, and fully functional when it comes to achieving this goal. Our role is to provide you with a leadership model coupled with the tools and systems you need to be an effective leader. It's your choice which aspects of this book you choose to implement as you grow your virtual meeting leadership skills.

If you are already a master at leading virtual meetings, *Lead Great Virtual Meetings* will provide additional insights that can further enhance your skills. If you are new to leading virtual meetings, The Six Principle Model reveals the steps you need to take to consistently lead great meetings and achieve outstanding results.

Chapter 1 Key Points

1. For the purposes of this book, a "virtual meeting" links two or more people in two separate locations via electronic or digital means. It includes conference calls, teleclasses, video conferencing, webinars,

classes delivered on Learning Management Systems (LMS), and on Avatar-Based-Platforms (ABPs). These may be synchronous (in real time) or asynchronous (recorded).

2. No matter which delivery platform you use, the success or failure of EVERY type of virtual meeting is rooted in what takes place in the auditory environment.

3. Your ability to engage and connect with participants is the foundation upon which all successful virtual meetings are built.

4. The Six Principle Model addresses who you are as a leader, how you will interact with those attending your meetings, plus how to handle the challenges you face leading in a virtual environment. It is the most important aspect of this book—the strategies, tips, and techniques are secondary.

Chapter 2:
The Six Principle Model

To lead people, walk beside them...
As for the best leaders, the people do not notice their existence.
The next best, the people honor and praise.
The next, the people fear;
And the next, the people hate...
When the best leader's work is done the people say,
"We did it ourselves!"
Lao Tzu

The Six Principle Model provides a powerful foundation for leading any type of meeting, whether it's online, by phone, or in person. As you go through each principle, remember they are designed to adapt to you, the type of meeting you are leading, and your personal strengths.

The Six Principles

The Six Principle Model was originally designed for leading effective interactive meetings in a conference call or teleclass environment. Over the years, however, we have discovered it works equally well with face-to-face meetings, webinars, online classes, and on interactive video meeting platforms such as Zoom. What changes in the virtual environment is more a matter of tactics rather than how you show up as the leader.

As you grow your leadership skills, you will continue to discover new ways to apply The Six Principles. The more you incorporate The Six Principles into your leadership style, the more effective you will be.

Principle #1:
People Listen for Their Reasons, Not Yours

Principle #1 is the foundation for all successful meetings. Even though your participants are physically present, are they really listening to you? If they're not listening, there's no learning, and no forward movement toward your goals. Instead, you get multi-tasking, resentment, and failure to implement on important items.

Warning signs you're not listening

While you may believe you're listening, if you are engaging in any of the following behaviors, you're not truly hearing what the other person is saying:

- Mentally preparing what you're going to say next.
- Interrupting the person who is speaking.
- Passing judgment (good or bad) about what is being said.

In order to enhance your connection and productivity in all types of meetings, there are two key questions to address.

- What would make this meeting so valuable that each person who attends would choose to be there rather than somewhere else?
- What would motivate each participant to take action once he or she leaves the meeting?

When you can answer these questions, your participants have a reason to listen to you.

To illustrate the importance of Principle #1, in 2005 I wrote a book called *Waging War on Real Estate's Discounters*. We had incredible sales and there was a tremendous demand for me as a speaker. The book, however, was highly controversial: The Department of Justice had issued strict guidelines about "commission fixing" in the real estate industry. The critical factor was using a specific percentage such as "six percent." As a result, not only were the attorneys for the company sitting in the room, if I was speaking for a state or local association, the attorneys for the discount brokers were also in the room waiting to pounce.

By working with the attorneys and other experts on the legal issues, I was able to customize my sessions to fit the specific clients' needs. I was surprised when a number of these attorneys said they had argued against bringing me in to speak but were happy with how the issues were covered. What surprised me most was the feedback from the attorneys for the discount brokerages: even their agents were being asked to discount their commissions!

Fast forward to how this principle applies to my business today.

When someone contacts me about speaking, I always tell them I want to customize the session to fit their needs and ask:

What challenges are you facing right now? Are there any burning issues that you or your group really would like me to address? Is there a specific message you would like me to convey?

Many people are taken aback by these questions. As we talk, however, they open up about their expectations and how we can best work together to achieve their goals.

It's equally important to discover what your participants' expectations are. Many top speakers visit with the early arrivers. After greeting them, they inquire about what motivated the person to attend. They also inquire about any questions they would like answered during the session.

These two steps have made a tremendous difference in both the quality of my sessions and the receptiveness of the room. The reason, of course, is Principle #1, people listen for their reasons, not yours.

Principle #2: People Support What They Help to Create

Principle #2 is critical to building engagement during your meetings. Strong engagement results in increased sharing of ideas, comments, and suggestions as well as an increased likelihood of participants taking action after the meeting. The more people contribute to the meeting and the more you acknowledge their contributions, the greater their commitment will be to taking action afterward.

In contrast, less effective leaders only focus on creating buy-in. Buy-in occurs when participants express support for a given idea or position. The most effective leaders measure their success by the actions their participants take, not by what they say they may do. A classic example is the person who agrees to contribute to a charity, but never gets around to writing a check.

Since 2007, I have used Principle #2 to determine the content for our Annual Awesome Females in Real Estate Conference. What's described next may seem a chaotic way to run a three-day conference with up to 50 speakers, but it has proven its effectiveness year after year. Here are the steps:

- Have 1:1 conversations with previous attendees. Inquire about the challenges they are facing, hot-button issues, and topics about which they would like to hear more. When a number of women express interest in the same topic, add that topic to the agenda.

- Based upon their response, set a theme. For example, before COVID-19 struck, we had already set our 2020 theme as "New Decade, New Directions." At the time, no one suspected how apropos that would be.

- Invite speakers who express an interest in addressing a specific aspect of each year's theme or who can contribute fresh insights to the challenges the group is experiencing, whether or not they have attended in the past.

- Search for what's fun or quirky. For example, a huge favorite was, "Men Are Like Waffles and Women Are Like Spaghetti," based upon a book addressing the differences in how men and women communicate. Our attendees found that simple distinction had broad application in both their business and personal communication styles.

During the 30+ years I have been in leadership, Principle #2, "People support what they help to create," has applied in almost every leadership situation I have encountered.

Principle #3:
Connection, Connection, Connection

Connection is the precursor to engagement. If you want to build more connection during your meetings, the most important shift you can make is from being "me-focused" to being "participant-focused."

This can be exceedingly difficult, especially when you first begin leading virtual meetings. Performance anxiety is common and for good reason. Not only do you need to be concerned about your content, you must also deal with the technology, how you come across in a virtual environment, and a variety of other issues that can reduce your connection with participants.

Nevertheless, the moment you shift your attention to how you look or what you want to say next, you miss what others have to say. This in turn reduces the connection during your meeting.

What's fascinating about Principle #3 is that when you focus on connection, many of the challenges you would normally face seem to magically disappear.

To illustrate this point, I've heard other professional speakers discuss how to handle "snipers" in the audience. These people typically sit about one-third of the way back, on the aisle, and to the speaker's right.

I've seen this in other speaker's sessions, but I can recall only one meeting almost 30 years ago where I had a sniper. I've certainly had people disagree with me or challenge what I say. When someone raises a valid point, I say, "Point well taken."

If the point isn't relevant, I often respond with, "Thank you," and then pivot back to the topic by asking the group, "Are there any other questions or comments?" If the issue is controversial or has the potential to break the connection within the group, I often invite the person to follow up with me after the session. They seldom do.

As Byron explains,

Connection is not about compromise, nor agreeing with people or their ideas. Instead, it's about giving people a chance to speak their minds, to speak their version of the truth, and to know that what they say has been heard. When your participants experience connection and feel that their viewpoint has been heard, they are more accepting when the group opts for an idea different from their own. In terms of group cohesiveness, what matters most is that they had their say.

When people are not heard, not only is the connection broken, they may also feel as if they're not an important part of the group. The result can be bitterness and frustration.

The Talking Circle: A powerful approach to building connection

For over 35 years, Marilyn Naylor was a close friend and mentor. Marilyn did extensive work inside the Native American community. She also played a huge role in helping me launch my Awesome Females in Real Estate conference. The most important lesson she taught me was how to conduct a "talking circle."

Native Americans and numerous other cultures use talking circles to create collaborative outcomes. Byron and I attended several Native American conferences where tribes from across Canada gathered in Vancouver, British Columbia. In every breakout and in the final joint session, there was a talking circle where everyone had their say.

Communities in the Netherlands have used talking circles to help drug-addicted youth by bringing the police, local leadership, and communities together to address the problem.

In my own career, I have used talking circles in my psychology classes, at my women's leadership conference, as well as with senior leadership in real estate and education. What's surprising is that talking circles are the equivalent of a face-to-face conference call.

Here are the guidelines for holding a talking circle in a face-to-face environment. (My personal preference is 8-15 in a circle, although I've seen groups as large as 300 at Native American gatherings.)

- You can only speak when you hold the talking stick.

- Pass the talking stick clockwise around the circle.

- Only share your experience. You cannot comment on what anyone else shares.

- If you're not holding the talking stick, keep your body language still and concentrate on what each speaker says.

- What is said in the circle, stays in the circle.

(You can find detailed instructions for holding a Talking Circle in Appendix B.)

The nature of your meeting determines the type of question to ask your "circle." For example, if you're leading a conference call or teleclass, you could ask participants what they would like to take from the meeting.

Another question that has worked well in business meetings, interactive teleclasses, and my psychology classes is, "What is one challenge you faced this year and how did you handle it?" This powerful approach can rapidly create strong personal connections even among strangers. One of my psychology students described his experience like this:

I felt more connected to the people in our circle in just 40 minutes than I do to people I've known all my life.

The reason is simple. Americans constantly talk over each other. In the talking circle, everyone listened and heard what each person said. It's a rare situation in most Western societies and the connection it creates can be profound.

Principle #4: Surface the Wisdom of the Group

Different people have different strengths and areas of expertise. It's extremely difficult to make good decisions when you have limited information and resources. Surfacing the wisdom of the group reminds the leader to tap into the collective experience, wisdom, creativity, and perspective of each individual. The challenge is how to do it.

The power of brainstorming

Brainstorming provides an excellent model for surfacing the wisdom of the group. Here are the steps to follow:

- When you begin the brainstorming process, explain the group is to focus solely on generating ideas rather than discussing or critiquing any specific idea.

- Gather as many ideas as possible. You will quickly discover the free flow of ideas sparks other ideas. As solutions emerge, they often become the springboard for even more ideas.

- Critically evaluate the ideas the group generated and identify which approach(es) are most likely to yield the best results.

- Select your action plan and begin implementation.

Because people are more accustomed to shooting down ideas rather than surfacing them, this shift can be challenging. The leader's role is to create a safe place for people to express their ideas without them being critiqued or put down.

On the other hand, it's still important to avoid "blue sky thinking" that fails to address what can go wrong. If you have someone who is really good at finding the flaws in what's being proposed, invite that person to identify potential pitfalls after you finish brainstorming. Always follow up by asking the other people in your group about what could go wrong as well.

Case Study

I was hired by the Williamson County Association of Realtors to conduct The Strengths Finder training session for their Texas Realtors Leadership Program. This program prepares Realtors to serve on their local or state board. As part of their training, the group had selected a challenge the association was facing and was tasked with coming up with a workable solution. Since this was my first time leading this session, I wanted to do something using The Six Principle Model that would also help the group be better prepared to tackle the long-term project they had selected.

Prior to the meeting, each Realtor took The StrengthsFinder assessment (from Tom Rath's book *StrengthsFinder*). Even though the group had been together for several sessions, I broke them into two groups of 12 to do a talking circle. I asked the two following questions:

- *Based upon The Strengths Finder Assessment, what are your two greatest strengths?*

- *What is the one role or task that is a poor fit for you?"*

Once they finished their circles, the two groups were to tackle a real-life challenge the Austin Board of Realtors (ABOR) faced when they decided to change Multiple Listing Service vendors. ABOR solicited individual member and company responses, held numerous meetings throughout the region, and still selected a vendor that didn't work out.

We asked each group to create a written action plan that included the following:

- The specific steps required to make the transition.

- The process for determining how the final vendor selection would be made.

- The role each team member would play.

- How the group would engage members in the decision-making process.

- A plan for implementing the process.

When we brought the two groups back together, the Association Executive (CEO) and I were amazed by how much they had accomplished in less than 50 minutes. Both groups created detailed workable plans that could have been employed immediately to begin the transition process.

Takeaways from the debrief included:

- Both groups felt strongly connected to their team and were energized about working together.

- They felt they had met the objectives set out for them and had a workable plan.

- They believed the best person on the team had been assigned to the role best suited to each individual's personal strengths.

- By knowing each person's individual strengths, they found it easier to delegate those tasks to the person best suited to handling them.

- They had determined which individuals could provide strong secondary support to each role when needed.

- They felt strongly the training had an immediate application to the long-term project they were to complete as part of their training.

- They also believed the approaches used in the training could be applied to future leadership challenges they would face.

As this case study illustrates, there's a wealth of wisdom sitting in the room, provided you "Surface the Wisdom of the Group."

Principle #5: Flex Your Flexibility Muscle

Due to COVID-19, many leaders, teachers, and trainers who knew how to function in face-to-face environments were thrust into leading virtual meetings. They had no leadership model to work from and little, if any training on how to use the technology. These newly minted leaders were forced to "flex their flexibility muscle" whether they liked it or not. So were their participants.

Leadership requires flexibility. This is especially true when it comes to dealing with the myriad of issues that occur in virtual meetings, whether it's the participants, the content, the technology, challenges within the organization, or any of the thousand ways your meeting can get derailed. In other words, you will have to constantly "Flex your flexibility muscle" to lead effectively, even when it's the same content on the same digital platform. Examples of adaptations you may have to make include:

- **Your delivery style**
  Is your meeting interactive? If so, what is the nature of the interactivity? Will you be interacting on a face-to-face platform like Zoom or Skype, on an audio-only conference call, or will you be limited to what participants enter into the chat function on a webinar or non-interactive video platform? How you build connection varies based upon the types of interactivity each platform accommodates.

- **Your content**
  In addition to your delivery style, you must also modify your content to fit both the delivery platform and the nature of the meeting. For example, if you're leading a conference call, expecting your participants to take detailed notes pulls their attention away from interacting. A better approach is to send out key written content before or after the meeting.

- **Group size**
  You can have a highly interactive meeting where every participant interacts at least once for groups of no more than 20 people. Beyond that, you'll be relying on input from only some of your participants.

- **Technology issues**
  Because they are usually outside your control, technology problems can be particularly frustrating. Furthermore, the larger the group, the more likely you are to have bandwidth issues, noise, and other types of distractions. If you're leading a large meeting or class, having someone available to handle the chat and any technology issues is one of the best strategies to minimize problems.

Select the leadership style you will use

Leading an effective virtual meeting begins with selecting the leadership style you will use for your meeting. You may be required to lead on a specific platform, but how you show up as the leader is up to you. Here's an example that illustrates key points to consider as you make this decision.

Picture yourself in a face-to-face meeting. Are you leading from the head of a long rectangular table or are you leading from a circular table? In the first case, you're leading from the front of room as the expert, the teacher, or the boss who is in control. In the second case, there's no head of the table. This approach makes it easier for you to lead from within the group where each person's ideas and suggestions are more likely to be heard.

This is especially important on audio-only meetings. When you do a content download or dominate the conversation, you're figuratively leading from the front of the room. In contrast, when you ask questions and truly listen, you begin building a safe environment where people interact and are more likely to take action after the meeting ends.

Leaders who rely on power and manipulation, typically have a strong need to be right or to show how smart they are. This approach creates an "I'm up, you're down" scenario. Up-down scenarios result in anger, resentment, passive aggressiveness, and sometimes even blatant resistance.

In contrast, when you lead from within the group, your focus shifts to the participants, the process, and the outcome. In most cases, leading from within the group produces the best outcomes. In fact, you may discover that once you are experienced with The Six Principles, your best meetings are those where you pepper in a few questions and your participants are actively engaged in discussion with each other. The sharing and brainstorming are intense and everyone leaves feeling excited about taking action.

Leading from within the group is also leading from the place of service. Robert Greenleaf coined the term "servant leadership" to describe this approach. As Lao Tzu observes:

To lead people, walk beside them...
As for the best leaders, the people do not notice their existence
When the best leader's work is done the people say,
"We did it ourselves!"

There are times when you must lead from in front of the group. When you use this approach, you are highly visible and will drive the process. In situations such as training, delivering directives from senior leadership, or other instances where specific information must be conveyed, there's really no other option.

When possible, "Flex your flexibility muscle" by leading from within the group. Fully engaging each person in the process strengthens their commitment to reaching the goal and increases the probability of your success.

Principle #6:
What You Do is What You Get

Participants model their behavior based upon what you do. When you're the leader, "Do as I say, not as I do" does not work. In other words, if you are snarky, your participants will be snarky. If you allow participants to be disrespectful to each other, they will be disrespectful to you. If you attempt to manipulate the participants, they will attempt to manipulate you or others.

On the other hand, if you are inclusive, your participants will be inclusive. If you acknowledge people for contributing, you'll see your participants acknowledge others as well. In short, whatever behaviors you exhibit during your meeting are the behaviors the other participants will exhibit as well.

Each participant brings their own expectations about what constitutes appropriate behavior during a virtual meeting. It's your role as the leader to model what you expect. Keep in mind that it may take time to fully implement The Six Principle Model and to eliminate inappropriate behaviors.

When something goes wrong, were you responsible for it?

If something goes wrong during your meeting, determine if something you did or did not do is the reason for the problem. Avoid blaming others, regardless of the issue.

Once you wrap up the meeting, use The Six Principle Model to uncover what went wrong. Once you identify exactly what happened, you can avoid making the same mistake in the future.

The challenging part for you as a leader is obtaining straight feedback on unconscious behaviors you demonstrate under stressful conditions. Once you have reliable feedback and can own the challenging behavior, improvement is only a few short steps away.

Remember, the behaviors you display during your calls are the behaviors your participants will emulate. It really is that simple.

Additional Fundamentals You Need to Know

Because each individual has different strengths and weaknesses, there is no "one right way" to lead great calls and meetings. Instead, it's a process of uncovering your strengths, developing those strengths, and constantly assessing what does and not work for you personally. Here are some additional ideas that will support you to apply The Six Principle Model more effectively.

- **Each person is a unique leader**
  This fundamental truth frees you from every "should" you may have about leading any type of group. Your unique leadership style is based upon your life experience, personality, values, beliefs, skills, training, and daily practice. It is as unique to you as your fingerprint. Be yourself. Always work to improve your skill set. Learn from others and adapt what they do to fit your style, but never lose sight of what makes you unique.

- **The Six Principles are designed to fit YOU, not the other way around**
  You are primary; the model is secondary. Each person will apply The Six Principles differently. Your task is to discover how the principles apply in your unique situation with your unique skill set. Each time you lead a call or meeting, you have the opportunity to discover precious information about what does and does not work for you.

- **Understanding The Six Principle Model is not the same as applying it**
  Understanding something is different from being able to apply your understanding during an actual meeting. Even though we have worked with these principles since the 1990s, we both continue to discover distinctions and subtleties we have never noticed before.

- **Let go of being in control**
  You're the leader and you're supposed to be in control, right? Here's the issue. When you focus on being in control, you are focused on yourself. The result is you're disconnected from the group. The more disconnected you are, the more likely your participants are to engage in multi-tasking and other

behaviors that can disrupt your meeting or class. Your challenge is to replace control with trust by focusing on building connection and alignment, which is what The Six Principles shows you how to do.

I personally experienced how powerful this approach is when I shifted my focus from control to building connection and engagement. My meetings and classes were more fun and engaging, and with that, my rankings and positive feedback also increased.

- **The power of "pause"**
  One of the most important tools for keeping your meetings on track is using the word "pause." When there is an issue during your meeting, whether it's the technology, background noise, or someone who is long-winded or disruptive, you can use the word "pause" to break away from the present conversation and address the issue.

  If a participant is the issue, especially if their behavior is damaging to the safe environment you're seeking to build, you can use "pause" to interrupt the behavior. For example:

  Jane, could I ask you to pause please? You made an interesting point about how to proceed going forward. I would like to get some additional feedback on that topic from the other participants. Who else would like to share?

Once you take a few shares, you can move on to your next topic.

- **Find your own path**
  What makes The Six Principles so exciting is also what can make them frustrating. What works well for one leader may not work well for someone else. Experiment with The Six Principles to see what works best in your unique situation. You can also use The Six Principles as your guide in determining what worked well on your calls and meetings as well as diagnosing problems that occur. Ultimately, the only barometer that matters is what works well for you and your participants.

Applying The Six Principle Model

Again, there is no right or wrong way to use The Six Principle Model. Instead, mastery comes from consistently seeking feedback and constantly working to upgrade your performance.

As you begin working with each principle, determine whether your participants are more or less engaged when you use it. Keep your focus on them and you'll quickly learn what does and does not work for your personal leadership style. Embrace all parts of the process—the successes, the mistakes, and the failures. Acknowledge your successes and use your mistakes and failures as a way to enhance your growth as a leader.

There will be times when a participant will attempt to undermine what you hope to achieve. Even in these situations, The Six Principles allow you to regain control while still maintaining a collaborative environment. No matter how many challenges, mistakes, or brick walls you may bump into, The Six Principles provide a road map for navigating what you may encounter.

Again, the Six Principle Model is designed to build on your personal leadership strengths. Expand on what works for you, eliminate what doesn't work, and constantly seek to become even more effective with the people you lead.

Chapter 2 Key Points

1. The Six Principle Model is a roadmap for leading more effective meetings and classes, whether it's online, by phone, or in person. The Six Principles are:

    #1. People listen for their reasons, not yours.

    #2. People support what they help to create.

    #3: Connection, connection, connection.

    #4: Surface the wisdom of the group.

    #5: Flex your flexibility muscle.

    #6: What you do is what you get.

2. The primary goal of The Six Principle Model is to build connection and engagement.

3. You are a unique leader. The Six Principle Model is designed to fit you, not vice versa.

4. Understanding The Six Principle Model is not the same as applying it. The model is like peeling an onion. The more you work with it, the more you will appreciate the true depth of the model and the critical role it plays in helping you build on your success and learn from your failures.

5. The Six Principle Model is your roadmap to navigating any challenges you may encounter. Take advantage of it.

Chapter 3: Challenges Leading in an All Auditory Environment

*The less you talk,
the more you're listened to.*
Abigail Van Buren (Dear Abby)

The foundation for leading effective virtual meetings begins with understanding the dynamics of the auditory rather than the visual environment. When it comes to conference calls and virtual meetings, the quality of the auditory is critical to your meeting's success. To understand why this is the case, exactly how long will you stay on a call when it keeps breaking up? The bottom line is that when the auditory is bad, people quickly become frustrated. When it's really bad, they leave.

Even if you're conducting a virtual meeting on a video platform such as Zoom, the auditory channel is still the most important. There are two reasons this is the case. First, many participants join virtual meetings by phone. Second, bandwidth issues are constant and widespread. If your audio keeps breaking up, one best practice is to have meeting participants turn off their cameras.

To illustrate this point, several years ago I led a webinar attended by over 1,400 members of the National Association of Realtors. About 35 minutes into the session, a thunderstorm knocked out my internet connection. I quickly dialed in from my landline and continued the webinar as an audio-only teleclass.

I briefly explained the issue with the storm and picked up where I left off. Because I sent the handout prior to the meeting, most participants were already using it to follow the discussion.

Here's what came as a real surprise. Although the last 25 minutes were audio-only, only a tiny percentage of participants left the meeting early.

We're Wired to Be Visual

What makes the auditory environment especially challenging is our brains are wired to be visual. Thirty percent of the cortex is devoted to visual processing as compared to only eight percent for touch and only three percent for auditory processing.

Because conference calls and teleclasses are completely devoid of visual cues, the transition to an all auditory environment is especially difficult for experienced speakers, teachers, and other leaders who normally work in a face-to-face environment. In the absence of visual and body language cues, the leader is forced to rely exclusively on speech patterns, frequency of participant response, and levels of engagement. In fact, new leaders often master our model more quickly because they haven't learned to rely on visual cues.

Generational Differences

Generational differences also play a major role. Because Baby Boomers spent their early years with the phone as their primary mode of distance communication, most are comfortable with all auditory environments.

In contrast, most Gen Xers and older millennials grew up text messaging and abhor the thought of having a conversation by phone. As a result, they have significantly less experience hearing and interpreting auditory cues.

By the same token, younger millennials and Gen Z who are more accustomed to using Snapchat, Facetime, Instagram Stories, and WeChat, also rely heavily on visual cues. TikTok is a prime example—the most highly ranked posts typically have a music background that matches the video content.

The success of these platforms results from our preference for visual as opposed to auditory-only content. In fact, numerous studies have shown that 83-85 percent of all Facebook and YouTube videos are watched without the sound.

Nevertheless, when it comes to leading ANY type of virtual meeting, the auditory feed is what matters most. Due to our text messaging culture, millions of young leaders have little or no experience dealing with all-auditory environments, especially when it comes to leading a conference call or teleclass. If you have experienced a poorly led conference call, you have already experienced much of what is included in the next case study. If you haven't experienced a conference call before, please note the behaviors described during this meeting reflect what takes place in millions of ineffective meetings every single day.

Monday Morning Blues:
The Anatomy of a Poorly Led Conference Call

What you're about to read may be painful, but it's even more painful to experience first-hand, especially if you're the person leading the meeting.

Bernice: *I arrive three minutes early for our call. I'm eager to hear from our New Vice President and about our goals for the next quarter. I open my email and begin checking messages while I wait.*

(Five minutes after the scheduled start time) I can't believe it—the call still hasn't started. Where is she?

VP: Hi, is anyone there?

Bernice: Good morning, I'm Bernice Ross from Austin, Texas.

(Six other people share their names and locations.)

VP: I know we're supposed to start at the top of the hour. Since we have five people who still haven't logged in, let's wait a little bit longer. The weather here in Chicago sure is awful. It seems like the snow is never going to stop.

Bernice: *Several other participants jump in to describe the weather where they are. I can't believe that we're supposed to kill time because other people are late. At least I got all my email handled.*

At eight minutes after the hour, the VP finally says,

VP: I guess we should get started. We have a lot to cover in today's session—sorry I was a bit late, but my previous meeting ran over.

Bernice: *Oh-oh—I can't afford for this meeting to run over. I have a hard stop at the top of the hour. Just about everyone else does too.*

VP: There are three new strategies that we will be implementing during the next quarter. Strategy #1…

Bernice: *At last, we're getting to what we really need to discuss.*

(About three minutes later, someone else joins the meeting. The call announcement feature is on and announces the person's name right when the VP is explaining one of the most important aspects of the first strategy.)

Late Caller: Hello—hello—Is anybody there?

Bernice: *Of course, someone else is here. We were on time. What the heck is all that background noise—are you in Grand Central Station?*

VP: Thanks for joining our meeting. Let me briefly review what we have just covered.

Bernice: *What? We're supposed to listen to the same material over again because the guy with all the background noise was late?*

(One minute later another person joins the call.)

Bernice: *No, no, no—I can't believe she's going over the same information for a third time. What was that book, "Death by Meeting?"*

Now there's an echo in addition to the other background noise. Did she forget about the "mute all" feature?

We're now 30 minutes into the call. We had our weather update, a repeat of the same information twice for the two latecomers, and we've only partially covered the first strategy we were supposed to address today.

That background noise is still really bad. I can barely hear what she is saying. Finally, someone speaks up.

Tim: There's a lot of background noise. Could you please mute everyone but yourself so we can hear what you're saying?

VP: Oh, I'm sorry. Sure, I can do that, but then I can't answer any questions that you might have as we go along. Is that OK with everyone?

Bernice: Yes! Finally, the background noise is gone! We're finally back to discussing the details of the first strategy, but she's going into so much detail there's no way she's going to get through the other two strategies. I wish she had sent out an agenda with the concepts rather than spending so much time on details that could have been handled in an email.

VP: Does anyone have questions?

Bernice: *No one is responding because we're all still on global mute.*

VP: You sure are a quiet group. No one has any feedback?

Bernice: *I text her we all are still on mute.*

VP: Oh, I'm sorry, I forgot to press the unmute.

Bernice: *The background noise is back and it's so bad, I can hardly think.*

Diane: Yes, I had a question about the timeline for implementing this first strategy.

VP: Who's speaking please? Sorry, but could you speak up—I can't hear you because of the background noise.

Diane: It's Diane in Chicago. Would everyone please mute your phone?

VP: Thanks Diane. That really helped. What was it you were asking?

Bernice: *Great question from Diane. I'm excited to learn more about the other two strategies, but we only have ten minutes before the top of the hour.*

VP: Here's the second strategy…

Bernice: *It's now two minutes before I have to leave. I wonder how late this call is going to run. She still hasn't started on the third strategy. I can't be late for my next meeting. I hate to be the first one to leave, especially since the call exit and enter feature is still on.*

Jim Morgan just exited the call.
Sally Johnson just exited the call.
Tim Barrett just exited the call.

VP: Oh, I didn't realize what time it is. I know we're not scheduled to meet again until next month. Let me get with my secretary and see if we can squeeze in another meeting before then. Have to go—I'm late for my next meeting. Bye everyone.

Bernice: *I can't believe we're going to have to schedule another meeting when everyone's schedule is already packed to capacity. How are we supposed to implement these strategies when we only covered a few minutes on Strategy #2, and didn't even get to Strategy #3? How are we supposed to take action on this if we have to wait until next month?*

Does this scenario sound familiar? Sadly, it illustrates why conference calls are rated as one of the biggest time wasters in business. Responses among the call/meeting participants can range from outright anger to complete numbness.

To make sure this doesn't happen to you, the next chapter addresses the fundamental technology basics you need to lead effective meetings.

Chapter 3 Key Points

1. When it comes to conference calls and virtual meetings, the quality of the audio is critical to your meeting's success for two reasons. First, many participants join video conferences from their mobile devices. Second, bandwidth issues may prevent you or your participants from being able to use the video feed.

2. Because our brains are wired to be visual, many leaders find leading in an auditory-only environment to be difficult.

3. The auditory-only environment can be particularly challenging for younger leaders who are accustomed to communicating via text message rather than talking on the phone.

4. Review the conference call transcript from this chapter. Can you identify how one of The Six Principles could have improved the call?

Chapter 4:
Technology Basics

*We are stuck with technology when what
we really want is just stuff that works.*
Douglas Adams

Technology is a challenge no matter what type of call or virtual meeting you are leading. You can have the best presentation or content in the world, but if the technology acts up, your meeting can quickly crash and burn.

Most webinars and online training/education platforms give you the option of accessing the meeting directly through the web or through a teleconference number with a pin code. Consequently, the following strategies apply any time participants can interact with voice, not just through the chat function.

TWO IMPORTANT CAVEATS:

1. To avoid relying on trial and error, please take the platform provider's training on their software. Lack of training on the provider's platform dramatically increases the problems you will encounter.

2. Be alert for platform upgrades, updates to your computer's operating system, and any other programs you use for content creation such as PowerPoint. Any one of these can result in changes to the default settings.

For example, when Zoom did a recent upgrade, I was in the midst of recording a new version of our *List and Sell Real Estate Like Crazy* online training. Prior to the upgrade, I had been using Zoom's "Original default" setting which fit the Digital Chalk Learning Management System (LMS) I was using to deliver our classes.

When Zoom upgraded their system, the default shifted from "Original" to 16:9. The result was half my videos had a big black space running the length of the screen between the slides and the presenters.

Also, whenever you upgrade your computer's operating system, check the computer's defaults, especially the audio. I logged on to lead a meeting with my co-host and I couldn't hear him. My Zoom settings were all correct. I finally checked my computer's system settings. The volume setting had defaulted to zero due to an OS upgrade the night before.

Pre-Meeting Technology Checklist

The following checklist provides a list of the key technology decisions you must make prior to leading most types of virtual meetings.

Pre-Meeting Technology

____1. Review the features and any special options your meeting host provides and decide which ones you will use.

____2. Decide the security level for your meeting and whether you want it to be passcode protected. (Change passcodes regularly if security is an issue. This is especially important if you're leading any type of meeting where attendance is open to people you did not personally invite or if the meeting is posted on the web.)

____3. If using a Moderator/Speaker PIN code and Participant PIN code, determine which participants will have access to which code. It's usually smart for at least two people to have the moderator code in case one person has a problem or is bumped off the meeting. Only the moderator can launch the meeting.

____4. If operator assistance is available during your meeting, write down the number to dial if you or the participants need assistance. (In some cases, there may be two different numbers.)

____5. Decide whether you will use global mute (lecture mode) vs. individual muting. If you elect to use individual muting, write down the instructions and be sure to explain to your participants at the beginning of each meeting how to mute their audio. For

Technology Basics

example, "Use your phone's mute function," or "Push *6 to mute yourself during the meeting."

____6. If you're leading a conference call, determine whether you will use the "Announce name" and/or the "Entry/Exit" tones at the beginning of your call. (Avoid irritating name announcements by turning this feature off once you formally start your meeting. Some leaders prefer to leave the entry/exit tones on while others choose to turn those off as well.)

____7. If the platform you are using has a chat function, post important links and information about obtaining tech support when you first start your meeting. Please note, late arrivers will only see what is posted in the chat from the point when they join the meeting. Consequently, you may want to repost any important information a second time later in the meeting.

____8. Avoid time zone confusion by providing the start time for one time zone only. If you are doing an international call, provide your preferred time zone and ask the participants to check https://www.timeanddate.com for the correct time for their area. (We normally use U.S. Eastern Time.)

____9. Compile the conference call number, passcodes, PIN codes, and other key instructions and send them out to your participants at least two days prior to the call. Send a second notice with the same information 24 hours prior to when the call is scheduled. It's smart to send a third notice 10-15 minutes before the call is scheduled to start. Participants appreciate the reminder, especially when it has the login instructions

To improve your leadership effectiveness, use the five guidelines outlined in the next section prior to every call/meeting you lead.

Hiss, Pop, Buzz, Snore: Minimizing Annoying Distractions During Auditory Meetings

With the drastic drop in the number of people using landlines to join conference calls, audio quality has deteriorated substantially from in the past. There are two important reasons. First, mobile devices regularly have spotty reception and drop calls. Voiceover IP (VoIP) is the second reason. If your phone service is tied to your internet service, your "landline" is a VoIP solution.

VoIP breaks up the audio and video into small packets of data, transmits them across the web, and reassembles them once they reach their destination. This is the reason your audio, which is what matters most, may be poor quality while your video quality is acceptable.

A second issue with VoIP is connection speed. VoIP solutions rely on the connection speeds of both the sender's and user's connection. Connection speeds vary tremendously depending upon the amount of web traffic on a particular hub. Even with fast connections, there are days when connections drop information because they are painfully slow.

Furthermore, even if you are on a fast connection, if you're sharing that connection with a number of people at your office or home, it can be as bad as a slow connection. This has become a fairly common occurrence, especially on Zoom and Skype meetings during heavy traffic times on the web. The result has been an increasing number of meetings to audio-only due to slow connections. This is another reason why you must be prepared to lead in an all auditory environment.

1. **Use the following steps to maximize sound quality during your calls and meetings**

   - Make sure that you are on a high-speed connection. If you need to upgrade your present service, do so.

   - Avoid leading from your mobile device unless there is no other option. If you're leading and your call is dropped for some reason, you may be unable to rejoin your meeting. This is an especially difficult issue if the platform you are using is programmed to end the meeting when you leave the meeting.

- Use a wired headset or microphone rather than Bluetooth. We have an on-going issue at our house when Byron uses his Bluetooth headset in his office. When I pull into the garage, the Bluetooth in my car grabs the call and links it to the vehicle's Bluetooth system. Byron is left wondering whose mobile device dropped the call.

- Experiment with different providers to determine which is best suited for your meetings. Alternatively, you can record your meeting or have someone else listen in to determine which platform provides the best audio quality.

As previously noted, when providers upgrade their systems, sometimes the quality declines rather than improving. Check your audio quality before every meeting. If there is an issue, determine if it is the provider, if it's due to the weather, or some other issue.

To illustrate this point, a leader on a recent virtual meeting was using her company's internal VoIP system. The audio portion of the meeting was so garbled that you could only understand about 40 percent of what she was saying. The company was about to launch a major international training initiative using this particular VoIP provider as the backbone of their system. I suggested recording a meeting and playing it back for her boss. They immediately changed providers.

2. **Avoid "talking down" to your participants**
   If you use the speaker phone function on your phone, you are not just "talking at them," you are literally talking down to them. (Note that when you use the speakerphone function, you lean down to speak towards the phone.) Unless your phone has noise cancellation, speakerphones amplify the background noise and substantially degrade the quality of your communication. If any of your participants must use a speakerphone, have them mute their side of the call to minimize background noise.

   To avoid a myriad of issues including annoying background noise, use a noise-canceling headset or microphone. Fortunately, most mobile phone headsets effectively block background noise. They also usually work with your computer. More importantly, rather than talking down to your participants you will be talking with them.

3. **Ignoring loud breathing, chewing, paper rustling, or other background noise**
   Sooner or later, leaders will bump into a serious background noise problem, or worse yet, the participant who wanders into the bathroom and forgets to mute the audio (or heaven forbid, the video!) There is no reason for you or your participants to tolerate background noise. While participants can blank out noise in their personal environment, it's virtually impossible to do so when the noise is coming over their phone, computer, or headset.

   There's nothing comical about someone breathing loudly, chewing, rustling paper, or even using the bathroom during your call and forgetting to use the mute. When this occurs, it almost always derails the call. To avoid having this happen to you, strongly advise your participants to call from a quiet environment and to self-mute unless they are speaking.

   If there is a problem, immediately stop the discussion. Tactfully point out that someone (ignore temptation to pinpoint blame) is breathing heavily into the receiver, is rustling paper, or whatever the issue may be. If you get any wisecracks, ignore them. Ask everyone (including you) to check the position of his or her receiver or headset. You can then return to the participant who was originally speaking. Do NOT assume that the noise will stop on its own. Take steps to deal with it immediately.

4. **"Hello, Hello, Hello"—controlling echoes**
   Echoes are the bane of conference calls, regardless of your leadership skills. Echoes are much more common on landlines. As mentioned earlier, the trade-off with mobile devices is dropped calls. With VoIP, it's video and auditory quality due to bandwidth and other issues.

   If you hear an echo during your meeting, ask the most recent caller(s) to hang up and call back. If you are working with an operator-assisted call, the operator may be able to identify which line brought in the echo. Sometimes muting the call works, but this eliminates interactivity. If you cannot eliminate the echo, the last resort is to have everyone hang up, wait 30 seconds, and call back. (This includes you.)

5. **Commercials and music on hold**
   Some participants call in from companies that play commercials or have music on hold. If a participant has this feature on their phone system and places you on hold, you have two options for handling the music/commercial. First, mute the offending party if you are able to do so. Alternatively, have everyone hang up, wait 30 seconds, and call back. No matter what approach you choose, the longer you wait to address the issue, the more participants you will lose.

We strongly recommend that you follow these guidelines. Failure to do so can quickly derail your audio-only meetings and impede your goals.

While these guidelines apply primarily to voice-only meetings, Chapter 5 addresses best practices that work across multiple delivery platforms.

Chapter 4 Key Points

1. To minimize technology issues and a host of other problems, always take your platform provider's training on how to use their software.

2. Always check your settings before each virtual meeting, especially your sound. System upgrades to the delivery platform you are using, your ISP, or your computer can cause the system to default to the original settings.

3. Use the Pre-Meeting Technology Checklist to guide you through the process of setting up your delivery platform prior to your meeting.

4. To minimize background noise and maximize the quality of your audio feed, use a wired headset rather than a blue-tooth headset, make sure you are on a high-speed internet connection, and deal with background noise issues the moment they occur.

Chapter 5:
Best Practices that Work
Across Multiple Delivery Platforms

There are no secrets to success.
It is the result of preparation,
hard work and learning from failure.
Colin Powell

Each delivery platform has benefits and drawbacks. Because the best practices vary from platform to platform, being aware of these differences is critical. Whenever possible, choose the delivery platform best suited to your content and leadership style.

For example, I was surprised to discover the best personal connections and engagement take place on conference calls and teleclasses. Here's how Byron explains it:

When you are holding a phone to your ear or listening to a call on a headset (NOT on a speaker phone), the speaker is in your personal space. So is every other participant on the call. In every other venue, including video and face-to-face, you are at least at an arms-length distance from each other.

When your boss, business, school, or some other situation dictates the platform you will use, like it or not, you must adapt to what works best in that venue if you want to be effective.

Twelve Guidelines to Follow on
Every Virtual Meeting

The following best practices work for almost all meeting platforms. The more of these you follow, the easier it will be for you to lead effective meetings.

1. **Expect the unexpected**
   When you're leading any type of conference call or virtual meeting a good rule to follow is, "Pray for sunshine, be prepared for

rain." Based upon our experience, about 20-25 percent of the webinars and online meetings have some type of issue. When something does go wrong, remember Principle #5, "Flex your flexibility muscle." The greater your flexibility, the more likely you'll be able to deal with whatever issue threatens to derail your meeting. The next four examples are just a few of the issues we have personally encountered during the last few months.

- **You have to reload the meeting software**
  I can't tell you how many times I have had to reload Go To Webinar, WebEx, Zoom, or other virtual meeting platforms because they did an update. This can also become an issue when you upgrade your software or operating system. Whenever this occurs, check your default settings to make sure nothing has changed. Also, be sure to test your sound and video before each meeting begins.

- **Troubleshooting 101: log in a second time**
  The moment you start having issues with a meeting platform, especially if you're leading a webinar or other meeting that uses slides, merely logging off and logging back on frequently resolves the problem. Other times, the issues may be due to the fact that your slides did not upload properly or there's an unidentified glitch that prevents the meeting host from hearing you or from sharing your screen.

  I recently guested on a podcast where I couldn't hear either of the hosts when I logged in. I tried unplugging my broadcast microphone and using my laptop's sound and that didn't work. We all tried logging in again. Finally, I decided to switch browsers and that solved the problem.

  This is another important reason that you should always log in 30 minutes early. If the platform you're using is acting up, you at least have time to troubleshoot the problem.

- **The "Live" social media platforms are prone to even more problems**
  To illustrate this point, I was a guest on a Facebook Live broadcast for a large company. There were two meeting hosts

in two different locations. BOTH hosts were bumped off the meeting. I ended being both the speaker and moderator for the 10 minutes it took for one of the hosts to rejoin the broadcast. Twenty minutes later when my portion of the meeting ended, the second host still hadn't been able to log back into the meeting. When I spoke with her afterwards, she told me how she frantically tried to get back into the meeting and was unable to do so.

A few weeks later, I was scheduled to speak at a virtual conference. My session was scheduled for late morning, but I logged on for the entire event. One of the two hosts was bumped off the meeting multiple times over the course of the morning.

When it was my turn to speak, my audio kept cutting in and out, even though I had a professional microphone, was on a wired ethernet connection, and everything was showing strong from my side. In retrospect, I kicked myself for not realizing that the moment there was a sound issue, I should have logged off and logged back on. As noted in the previous example, however, sometimes you can't get back on the meeting.

As a rule of thumb, regular meeting platforms including webinar platforms, Skype, and Zoom are more stable and reliable than "going live" on the social media platforms.

- **The delivery system goes bonkers**
We have used the same conference calling system for over 15 years. Byron was recently scheduled to lead a group coaching call for one of our corporate clients. When he dialed into his normal number and used his password, it didn't work. He repeatedly tried to login and each time the system told him his password and login was not valid. The meeting would not start until he logged in with his moderator pin number. I suggested using my landline (actually a VoIP phone), but he had issues figuring out how my headset worked with my system.

I tried logging in as a participant and was able to do so. Ten minutes after this fiasco started, the system started working again and he was able to lead the call with the participants who patiently waited for him to arrive.

2. **Arrive early: the meeting actually starts when the first person arrives**

   No matter what type of meeting you are leading, engaging your participants as soon as they join the meeting is critical. Start the meeting off right and you have their attention. Start the meeting off wrong and both your engagement and attendance will plummet.

   If you're leading a conference call, arrive 5-10 minutes early. In most cases, you will have at least one other early bird on the call. Arriving early allows you to avoid the adrenaline that comes from being late for your own call. It also allows you to take charge of the call from the onset.

   If you're conducting a webinar or video-based meeting, arrive at least 30 minutes early in order to troubleshoot technical glitches as well as engage with early arrivers.

3. **How to welcome people to the meeting**

   If you are leading a small conference call or meeting, greet the people as they join by saying: "Welcome, this is Mary Smith. Who just joined the call?"

   If you have new participants you have not met before, state your name and the purpose of the meeting. For example, "Welcome to our third quarter update. This is Mary Smith. Who just joined the call?"

   If you are leading a large conference call or virtual meeting where it's impossible to greet each participant, begin by generically welcoming everyone to the call or meeting.

   Please note you CAN begin building engagement with those who arrive early. Here are some ways to do it.

   - If you're leading an interactive conference call, ask about challenges they're facing or what they would like to take away from the call or meeting. This approach allows you to immediately begin building connection plus it creates the impression that you are well prepared.

- If you're leading a large meeting or webinar, you can engage in conversation with the early arrivals by unmuting them individually or using the chat if available.

4. **Large meetings benefit from having a speaker and host/tech person**

   For large meetings, it's smart to have a co-host and/or tech person to run the chat function and to handle technical difficulties.

   If you are a guest on someone else's call or meeting, the host may have specific instructions about how they want to begin the meeting. Sometimes the host handles the greeting. Other hosts may engage you in a conversation to avoid having dead space before the call begins.

   If the host is unaccustomed to engaging early arrivers, you could suggest posting a pertinent question about challenges or other issues they may be facing in the chat. While voice or video engagement is preferable, you are following Principle #1, "People listen for their reasons, not yours."

5. **Never use these words!**

   "We're just waiting for a few more people to show up" or "We'll begin in a few minutes." This devastating mistake undermines both novice and experienced leaders right at the beginning of the call or meeting. Regardless of who is there, start on time. Again, your meeting begins the moment the first person arrives.

6. **Engage your participants right from the beginning**

   After you greet your participants, begin your call or meeting with a powerful question. Write this question down and make it 10 words or less. This approach immediately engages your participants and creates forward momentum in terms of accomplishing your agenda. Those who are on time will love that the call is on topic and moving. As late arrivals join the meeting, they realize they may have missed something important. This increases the likelihood they will be on time for future meetings.

7. **End on time**
   Ending your meeting on time is a must. This is especially important for most men. Research shows that men view time differently from women. Men are much more likely to become upset if you do not end on time because they haven't allocated additional time for your meeting. (This is true for many high drive women as well.) Failure to end on time can result in frustration and anger among your participants. The bottom line is avoid starting or ending late.

8. **For interactive calls and meetings, say your name first**
   This may seem like an unnecessary suggestion, especially if your meeting is among colleagues who know each other. Nevertheless, it's easy to confuse voices, especially on meetings with more than five or six people.

   Failure to say your name first, especially if there is someone new on your meeting, can create a sense of "Ins" (those who know everyone and recognize their voices) and "Outs" (those who don't know everyone).

   In addition to helping your participants stay connected with each other, this rule also prevents anonymous sniping at you or other participants. Having participants say their name first also makes it easier for everyone to track comments. This in turn improves your communication within the group while also increasing your effectiveness.

   It's extremely important to introduce this concept at the beginning of your first interactive call or meeting and whenever someone new joins your group. Remember Principle #6: "What you do is what you get." If you want people to say their name first, you must first model this behavior yourself. In fact, Byron has this habit so embedded in his behavior that he sometimes says, "Byron here" when he's on the phone with his immediate family.

9. **"Pause:" the most important word in your meeting vocabulary**
   Whether it's a problem with the technology or a participant who has gone off on a tangent, "Pause" is the most important word

you can use to keep your agenda on track. In fact, it's equally powerful in face-to-face meetings as well.

"Pause" allows you to instantly eliminate issues when they first occur. For example, if someone has joined the meeting late and brings in an echo, you can ask whoever is speaking to "pause." Next, ask the late arriver to rejoin the call or meeting to clear the echo.

If someone is derailing the meeting by going off on a tangent say, "Kim, will you pause for a moment? We were discussing XYZ topic. Do you have anything to add to that?"

"Pause" is also particularly effective when someone is rambling on too long. Ask, "Mark would you please pause? Could you sum up the point you were just making in a single sentence?"

A slightly different way to cope with a rambling participant is to highlight something he said as being important by saying, "Mark, that's an excellent point you raised about XYZ. I was wondering if anyone else has something to add to Mark's point?"

CAVEAT:

When using "pause," keep your voice and tone neutral. Avoid letting any anger or frustration about the situation creep into your voice when you say, "Pause." Failure to follow this guideline can damage your connection and result in anger and hostility.

10. Avoid randomly calling on participants

Rather than building connection and trust on your meeting, randomly calling on meeting participants often creates fear and uncertainty. This in turn can result in passive aggressive behavior. It also discourages creativity, productivity, and teamwork.

If you doubt this, think back to a time in school when a teacher randomly called on students. You hated it then and your participants hate it still.

In situations where you need a response from every participant, use the following approach: "I would like to hear from everyone on the call/meeting. Who would like to lead off?"

If you still haven't heard from two people, you can say, "Sue and Don, I haven't heard from you. Which of you would like to go first?"

11. Question, question, question

Asking open-ended questions (i.e. questions that start with the words, "What" or "How") is one of the most powerful ways to engage your participants. Avoid using the word "why" because it puts the other person on the defensive.

If possible, ask a question that taps into the person's strength and is relevant to accomplishing the call/meeting agenda. Once you ask the question, you must fully listen to what is being said. Your role as the leader is to help determine how each person's input relates to accomplishing the stated goal of the meeting.

12. Take notes the old-fashioned way—write them down

While you may be faster on a keyboard, typing can be a distraction, especially if you have a good microphone and your participants can hear you typing while you're supposed to be focused on leading. Consequently, it's better to take notes by hand.

At the time we went to print, Otter.ai is an excellent transcription service offering up to 10 hours of free transcription services per month.

You can use Otter in two ways. You can record your meeting directly on Otter and it will transcribe the meeting in real time. Alternatively, if you recorded on some other meeting platform, upload the audio/video into Otter and it will create the transcript.

Reading the transcript is much faster than listening to the playback of the entire meeting. Moreover, the transcript is searchable. Where the transcript is unclear or in error, click on the text in the transcript and Otter plays back the recording.

CAVEATS:

There are two caveats here. While people who attend online classes or webinars expect those sessions to be recorded for playback later, this is not necessarily the case for most conference calls. If you are recording a meeting, advise all participants prior to and again at the beginning of the meeting you will be recording the call.

Also, avoid becoming lax about taking your own notes. I made that mistake at a recent conference where I used Otter to transcribe the sessions in real time. I discovered my retention and recall of important meeting points was much poorer than normal. Furthermore, there's always the risk there will be a problem with the recording (which there was).

Follow these 12 guidelines to increase the productivity and the effectiveness of your calls and meetings. In the absence of best practices, you are back to relying on trial and error. Your role as a leader is to maximize the effectiveness of each person. To lead the most effective call or meeting possible, outline the behaviors you expect, ask great questions, and focus on building connection and engagement.

Chapter 5 Key Points

1. About 20-25 percent of the time there will be a technology or some other major issue during your virtual meeting. When that happens, be prepared to utilize Principle #5, "Flex your flexibility muscle" to quickly troubleshoot the problem.

2. Always arrive early for your meeting. For conference calls, 10 minutes early is usually sufficient, but for meetings using video or slides, arrive at least 30 minutes early.

3. Always start on time and end on time.

4. Engagement and the opportunity to build connection begins the moment your first participant arrives at your meeting. Take advantage of it.

5. "Pause" is the most important word in your meeting vocabulary. When you use "Pause," always use "charge neutral."

6. Use "how" and "what" questions to keep participants engaged.

Chapter 6:
Issues to Address Before Your Video-Based Virtual Meeting

*One of the key qualities a leader must possess is the ability
to detach from the chaos, mayhem, and emotions in
a situation and make good, clear decisions
based on what is actually happening.*
Jock Willink

The Six Principles tackle how to lead effective interactive meetings. Fortunately, most of the principles also apply to virtual meetings even when there is little or no interaction. As in the conference call model, there are plenty of resources that explain how to set up your virtual meeting, how to attract participants, as well as how to avoid technology pitfalls.

Nevertheless, the same challenge still exists: these models are not leadership models. In truth, the real key to the success of your video-based class, meeting, or webinar depends more upon who you are as a leader and the quality of the connection you create with your participants. In fact, your participants will forgive almost anything, provided you have established a strong connection with them.

While much of what follows applies in both business and academic settings, this chapter focuses primarily on leading virtual meetings and classes in a non-academic setting. Chapter 11 addresses specific issues related to leading virtual classes in an academic setting including using a Learning Management System (LMS) and Avatar-Based-Platforms (ABPs).

Different Platforms, Different Strategies

When you make the move from face-to-face to a virtual meeting platform, the presentation dynamics change dramatically. What works well in face-to-face meetings often does not translate well on virtual meeting platforms. The reason is simple. When you're presenting face-to-face, you not only have your slides and voice to work from, you also have your body language, the stage/meeting room, the visual and body language feedback from the participants, plus a host of other variables that are missing in the virtual meeting format.

As mentioned earlier, regardless of the type of meeting you're leading, the audio is what matters most. You can get by without the video, but if there is an issue with the audio, your meeting/class is over. This is why we placed so much emphasis on the conference call model first. The audio feed is paramount. Your ability to engage your participants is what will make or break the effectiveness of your virtual meeting.

Six Primary Methods for Delivering Content

Here's how the six primary methods for delivering content differ.

1. **Face-to-face**
   In the face-to-face environment, you have both rich auditory and visual feedback. If you're paying attention, you can easily tell whether the people in the room are bored, engaged, or tuning out. When someone asks a question, their voice provides a host of auditory cues as well. It's easy to determine whether the person is asking for information or is attempting to undermine your position in the room. Meeting in a single location minimizes the amount of external distractions you will experience.

2. **Auditory-only**
   On auditory-only meetings, whether it's a conference call, a teleclass (training delivered via telephone) or any virtual meeting/class without a video feed, you lose the visual component. Instead, you must rely exclusively on auditory clues. This is especially challenging for speakers, teachers, and subject matter experts who unconsciously depend upon visual cues to read the room. It's also a challenge for younger leaders who seldom speak on the phone. Instead, they're used to communicating through text messaging. As a result, many younger leaders lack the ability to read tone, inflection, and other verbal cues that are critical in the auditory environment.

3. **Video-based virtual meetings and classes**
   Having the video feed on during your meeting is a two-edged sword. On the one hand, you can see those in attendance which means you have access to a wide variety of visual cues. On the other hand, you also have the audio feed from multiple sources. It takes only one unmuted participant to answer a phone call to completely derail your meeting.

   Complicating matters even more, instead of having a single location where all the participants are together, you're seeing a different location for each participant. It's much easier to control the distractions in a single room as opposed to multiple rooms where the distraction factor increases exponentially, even when you have their audio feed turned off.

4. **Webinars**
   Webinars are one of the most difficult types of meeting to deliver because you are often the speaker, the moderator, and the technician all wrapped up in one. This is the formula for a disaster if anything on your webinar goes wrong. You can't keep people engaged and handle technical issues at the same time.

   The difficulty increases when you elect to drop the interactive components of the webinar such as the chat, polling, and other interactive features. Without these features, you'd be delivering a monologue. While having a strong slide deck can help, having two or more voices on the webinar works much better. Even the most talented radio talk show hosts generally have callers or guests on their shows. A conversational approach is one of the best ways to keep your audience engaged.

5. **Learning Management Systems (LMS)**
   A robust LMS provides a wide variety of benefits which we will discuss in Chapter 11. Unless you are delivering live on the LMS, it has the same drawbacks as leading a webinar. Even so, you can still build a rich array of interactive elements into your meetings and classes even when they're recorded.

6. **Avatar-Based-Platforms (ABPs)**
   Avatar-Based-Platforms such as Second Life and Virbela are hybrid delivery systems that combine aspects of gaming technology, webinars, and video conferencing. As with any other virtual meeting platform, the audio is still primary. Depending upon which features you activate, you can run your ABP session as an interactive teleclass, like a webinar where you're engaging participants with the hand raise feature, or like a Zoom meeting where the speaker's slides and/or videos are displayed on an embedded screen in the "meeting room."

What Tools and Systems Will You Need?

You can have amazing content, but that only matters if you're able to deliver it effectively via the platform you use. The following checklists will guide you through the decision-making process required to put the right tools and systems in place for your meeting or class.

Tech Decisions You Must Address

Successful virtual meetings begin with the technology decisions you make. If you're doing this using your account, you will be responsible for deciding which of the following items you will use and how you will use them. If you're not using your own account, you will only have to handle the decisions outlined in items 6-10.

1. Which delivery platform will you use? If you are using a platform for the first time, take the provider's training on their platform as soon as possible.

2. Will you use a registration page? If so, be sure to include the title of your meeting, the host's name, date, time, instructions for registering, and a means of tracking who has registered.

3. Will you have a separate website or other location where you can post a link to the registration page and the meeting replay if applicable?

4. Will you utilize an automated system for sending email confirmations and post-meeting follow-ups?

5. If you are charging for the meeting, will you use a shopping cart or some other means for collecting payment?

6. Leaders need a high-speed internet connection with an ethernet and/or broadband connection if available. Conduct a "speed test" to identify which areas in your home and/or office have the fastest connection speeds. Avoid leading from your cell phone unless there is no alternative.

7. Will you use a separate camera or the built-in camera on your laptop or mobile device?

8. If you are not using your device's built-in camera, will you use a tripod or some other means to position your camera where you are looking directly at your participants?

9. If you are using a mobile device, we strongly recommend that you use a wired external microphone to reduce background noise and to achieve better sound quality.

10. If possible, use wired headphones rather than a Bluetooth headset.

Logistics

Again, you are responsible for all the decisions if you're leading a meeting or class from your own account. If you're leading for someone else, they will probably have items 1-5 handled and will advise you of what their expectations are. In terms of items 6-12, you must be able to answer the following questions that address what is expected of you as the leader.

1. What is the date and time for the meeting?

2. How long will the meeting be?

3. What type of virtual meeting will you be conducting?

4. How many attendees do you anticipate?

5. Will the meeting be free or fee-based?

6. Will someone be available to handle technical glitches other than the presenter and the moderator?

7. Will you use polling?

8. Do you intend to use the chat?

9. If you decide to use the chat, will only the moderator/speaker be able to see what is posted or will all posts be visible to all participants?

10. What portion of the meeting will be devoted to content and how much to Q&A?

11. Who will be responsible for setting up polls and/or monitoring Q&A?

12. Will participants be able to communicate with you after the meeting and if so, how?

Content Decisions

In most cases, you will be in charge of creating your own content, even if you have been given a specific topic to deliver. Here are some key questions to consider. (Chapters 7 and 11 contain an in-depth discussion about how to create highly engaging content that creates the greatest impact.)

1. What is the topic?

2. Who is the intended audience?

3. What is the title?

4. Will you use a deductive or inductive approach to presenting the content?

5. Will you review the goals/learning objectives for the session at the beginning of your meeting?

6. How many slides will you use?

7. Will you provide a written agenda, notes, or handout participants can download prior to, during, or after your meeting?

8. Will you review key takeaways at the end of your meeting?

9. After the meeting, what action steps do you want participants to take?

Fifteen Best Practices to Follow as You Plan Your Meeting

1. **Determine the approach you will use to cover your topic**
   The topic you select influences all aspects of your content creation. Some meeting leaders prefer a survey approach where they cover a wide number of topics within a single meeting. If you use this approach, be thorough enough that your participants will walk away feeling you did an adequate job of addressing each topic.

   A different approach is to take a single topic and to cover it in depth. This approach is especially useful if you are delving into a new product or helping people acquire a new skill.

   If you really want to become skilled at virtual persuasion, study the infomercials on late night TV. They introduce what they're selling, provide experts to support their claims, and then have a real-world demonstration of how their product works. From there, they have additional testimonials.

   While you may not be interested in selling anything, this model still provides an excellent way to delve into your topic in more detail. Putting it a little differently, the best virtual meetings not only provide actionable content, they also inspire participants to take action.

2. **Identify your intended audience**
   The easiest virtual meetings to lead are those where your audience is homogeneous. For example, it's much easier to lead a virtual meeting for a group of top-producing salespeople than for a group where the experience levels range from novice to expert. Consequently, make sure your description states the intended audience as well as whether the topic is best-suited for a general or specific audience.

3. **Specify the benefits participants will gain from taking part in your meeting**
   Virtual meetings fall into one of three major categories: training/education, "how to" product demonstrations, and meetings designed to sell a product. No matter what type of meeting you conduct, be sure to state the specific benefits each attendee will gain by enrolling. Training and other types of educational classes typically require learning objectives you outline at the beginning of your meeting as well as key points you review again at the end of the meeting.

4. **Decide on the time**
   As a rule of thumb, the best times to conduct your virtual meetings are between 11:00 a.m. and 2:00 p.m. on Tuesday through Thursday.

5. **Create an attention-grabbing title using the American Marketing Institute's Headline Analyzer**
   Having a strong title for your virtual meeting can definitely help you build attendance. Unfortunately, this is often easier said than done. One option is to hire a professional copywriter.

   A better option is to use the Headline Analyzer from the Advanced Marketing Institute (https://www.aminstitute.com) Their "Headline Analyzer" not only allows you to quickly evaluate the strength of your virtual meeting titles, it also allows you to evaluate any headlines you may use elsewhere in your business including on your blog, social media sites, YouTube, and print marketing materials.

The analyzer uses three different dimensions to assess the effectiveness of your title and headlines: intellectual, emotional, and spiritual. Depending upon the nature of your virtual meeting, you can quickly identify what will be most appealing to your target audience.

In terms of scoring, well-written headlines from professional copywriters usually range between 25-50. Exceptional headlines fall between 50-75.

I've been working with the Headline Analyzer for many years. Although their algorithms may change, the following guidelines can help you create the strongest title possible:

- Use the words "you" or "your" whenever possible. Avoid "I" and "me."

- Use commands rather than statements.

- Use a number in your title, preferably an odd number.

- Use the word "these" rather than "the."

- Use the words "strategies" and "secrets."

Here are some examples of how the Headline Analyzer works:

- "How You Can Stop Procrastinating in Your Life" scores a very respectable 28—professional copywriter quality.

- "How to Stop Procrastinating" scores at the top end of professional copywriter quality with a 50.

- Adding a number to your headline/title increases it even more: "Use These Five Strategies to Stop Procrastinating" scores a whopping 71. The secret here is to use a number (odd numbers are usually better than even numbers). In most cases, adding a number to your headline will increase your score substantially.

You can improve your ability to write great headlines and titles simply by monitoring your results.

6. **Customize your landing page and registration form**
Creating a customized landing page for your meeting can immediately engage participants while also driving registration. If you're leading for an institution or organization other than your own, it's common practice for the meeting organizer to request that you write this copy. Be sure to proofread very carefully, because this content may also be posted on the meeting organizer's registration page, in emails to potential participants, and in print as well.

7. **Additional ways to increase registration**
   - List at least three benefits participants will gain from attending your virtual meeting.

   - To generate engagement on your registration page, ask, "What topics/questions would you like to see addressed during this meeting?"

   - Create a "call to action," that also uses a benefit. For example:

   If you're ready to stop procrastinating register for, "Five Secret Strategies to Help You Stop Procrastinating Now."

   This headline received a "55" on the Headline Analyzer.

8. **Decide what to display on your "Welcome Screen"**
It's important to have a "Welcome Screen" that people see when they first join the meeting. This typically includes the title of your presentation, the name of the presenter(s), and if applicable, the name of the organization hosting the meeting. It also should mention that, "The meeting will be starting soon."

9. **When will you begin your content, at the top of the hour or two minutes after?**
   As a rule of thumb, begin your content about two minutes after. This gives those who login at the top of the hour time to punch in the passcodes and to download the meeting software if necessary. You can use the first two minutes to introduce the speakers/moderators and to review the housekeeping and other details for participating in the meeting.

10. **How you will be introduced?**
    As mentioned earlier, write an introduction of no more than 150 words. Again, nothing starts your meeting off on the wrong foot more than a lengthy list of all of your accomplishments. Always remember, your participants are focused on "What's in it for me?" (WIIFM)

11. **In addition to the speaker, have an organizer/moderator whenever possible**
    If you're delivering the meeting content, it's smart to have a moderator and/or another organizer. Moderators typically handle the introduction(s), cover the housekeeping details, and any other logistics. On large meetings, it's common for companies to have a third person who handles login problems or any other technology issues that occur during the meeting.

    If you're a guest speaker in a series, the moderator generally mentions the next meeting in the series at the beginning and the end of the meeting. If there is a sponsor, you will begin your content after the host or the sponsor says a few words about the sponsor's product. Be sure to thank the sponsor at the beginning and the end of the meeting and to adjust the length of your meeting accordingly.

12. **Handling the back-and-forth between co-presenters**
    If you are co-presenting, be sure to conduct a practice session prior to the meeting. This allows you to practice your transitions back-and-forth as well as working through any logistical issues.

13. Polling guidelines

Polling creates engagement. There are several issues to consider:

- How many polls will you conduct? If your meeting is one hour in length, a good rule of thumb is no more than 2-3 polls.

- Use a poll early in the meeting to drive more participant engagement.

- If you have a moderator or co-presenter, who will be responsible for opening the poll and reporting the results?

- What type of questions will you ask? For example, will you ask a question that solicits participants' opinions, helps participants understand something about themselves or the content, or pertains to their behavior in a given situation? Multiple-choice questions are usually more effective than "yes-no" or "true-false" questions.

- How long will you leave the poll open? Approximately 1-2 minutes is the right amount of time depending upon the size of the group and the question asked. Whatever you decide, announce when the participants have 30 seconds left to respond and then again when they have 10 seconds left. When you get to zero seconds, announce the poll is now closed and share the results.

- If your meeting platform allows both the organizers and the participants to see the poll results, display the final result as a percentage rather than the raw results. The reason? It can be very disconcerting to conduct a poll and only have a small percentage of people participate.

14. Tracking audience engagement

Some meeting platforms allow you to track audience engagement using an "attentiveness meter." "Attentiveness" can be tracked by monitoring who is raising questions in the chat, responding to polls, or who has minimized the meeting window to do something else. If your attentiveness meter drops to 30 percent or less, re-engage the audience with a question, poll, quiz, story, or video.

15. **Determine whether participants can view what's posted in the chat**

    There is no single best answer to this question. Some leaders prefer to keep the comments in the chat private (i.e., only the leader/moderator sees them) while others are comfortable displaying them for everyone.

    A few days prior to writing this chapter, I spent three days attending the first virtual conference held by *Inman News*, the real estate industry's leading news provider. The final conference session was a town hall devoted to gathering feedback about how to make any future virtual conferences they conduct better.

    Overwhelmingly, the Inman attendees wanted to have the chat available to share comments and resources during the session and to also be available on the replays.

CAVEAT:

Make sure all comments appear only on the meeting platform, not on a third-party platform such as Facebook, Google, LinkedIn, or YouTube. Having any participant leave your site to visit a third-party platform breaks your connection and is confusing for your participants.

Case Study
Using Polling to Ramp Up Interactivity

A few days before finishing this book, I attended a breakout session at Inman's Connect Now conference where the two leaders used polling in an entirely different way to "surface the wisdom of the group." In their 45-minute session, they conducted eight polls. When the breakout session was over, I felt like I had attended a very well-run teleclass. Here's what they did.

1. They prepared eight different questions and created a poll for each question.

2. After they shared the results of each poll, they discussed key takeaways about how this point could help participants with their businesses.

3. They also asked for feedback in the chat on each point.

4. They invited participants who wanted to unmute their audio to do so and share their feedback.

5. The meeting was fast paced, fun, and packed with useful takeaways.

Chapter 6 Key Points

1. The six primary types of meetings include:

    - Face-to-face.

    - Auditory-only meetings, i.e., conference calls and teleclasses.

    - Video-based virtual meetings on platforms such as Microsoft Teams, Skype, and Zoom.

    - Webinars.

    - Synchronous and asynchronous meetings and classes on Learning Management Systems.

    - Synchronous and asynchronous meetings and classes held on Avatar-Based-Platforms such as Second Life and Virbela.

2. Each delivery platform has unique benefits and drawbacks. If you have the option of selecting the platform you will use, carefully weigh each option to determine the platform best suited to your delivery style and the type of content you will be delivering.

3. There are three detailed checklists outlining key decisions you must address prior to leading your next virtual meeting. These include:

- Ten technology decisions.
- Twelve logistical decisions.
- Nine content decisions.

4. Carefully review the "Fifteen Best Practices to Follow as You Plan Your Next Virtual Meeting" as well. The more of these you can implement, the more effective your meeting will be.

5. To avoid becoming overwhelmed, begin with the items that are most applicable to the type of meeting you will be leading and are the easiest for you to implement.

Chapter 7:
How to Create a
High Impact Presentation

Entrepreneurs must be practical experts. They needn't set out to be subject matter experts in what they do; they must set out to solve a problem or pursue some cause or purpose greater than themselves.
Anne Sullivan

When you switch from leading face-to-face to leading virtual meetings, the presentation dynamics change dramatically. The reason the face-to-face model does not translate well into the virtual meeting model is simple. When you're presenting face-to-face, you not only have your slides and voice to work from, you also have your body language, the stage, the visual and body language feedback from the audience, plus a host of other variables that are not present in the virtual meeting format.

As mentioned repeatedly, the audio feed is primary in ALL virtual meetings. If you are leading any meeting using video and there are 10 or more participants, it's common for at least one of them to have a slow connection that causes the audio and/or video to break up. The simple fix is to have them turn off their video feed. They can still view you and the other participants, but you cannot see them. Again, this is why we recommend learning how to lead a great conference call or teleclass before tackling the webinar or other video-based meeting format. Your ability to engage your participants is what will make or break the effectiveness of your virtual meeting. Slides alone are not enough.

While the audio matters most, effective visuals still play a pivotal role in creating a high impact presentation. The "magic" happens when you have great audio coupled with great visuals. This requires careful planning based upon the platform you select, your purpose, the results you hope to achieve, and the action steps you want participants to take after the meeting.

Four Major Types of Virtual Meetings

The first step in creating a high impact presentation is to identify the type of meeting you will be leading. There are four major categories.

1. **Education or Training**
   Training and education meetings increase the participant's knowledge of a given topic. The best meetings go beyond knowledge acquisition by also providing the motivation, strategies, and systems necessary for the participants to complete assignments and/or take action after the meeting ends.

2. **Influence**
   Meetings designed to influence participants exist in a wide variety of environments. For example, a nurse may lead a meeting explaining why it's important for diabetics to monitor their blood sugar regularly and the risks of failing to do so. Professional speakers often hold webinars to influence participants to visit their website to learn more about their services. An executive whose sales team is behind on their quotas could have the team meet virtually to share best practices and report back at their next meeting about what worked and what didn't work.

3. **Inspire**
   Inspirational meetings exist to help others have a better life. For example, a minister might share his insights about resolving family conflicts in a virtual meeting format. Alcoholics Anonymous, Parents without Partners, and grief counseling groups seek to inspire those struggling with difficult life issues by hearing from others who are coping with similar challenges. Today, many of these meetings are taking place using a virtual meeting format.

4. **Sell**
   For meetings that sell to be effective, the leader must incorporate all three other meeting types:

   - Educate participants about what their product or service offers.

- Influence participants that the leader's product or service can help solve a problem or issue they face.

- Inspire participants to purchase the product or service.

What's the Purpose of Your Meeting?

Before making any decisions about the content of your meeting, you must first ask, "What is your purpose?" Another way of asking this question is, "What actions do I want participants to take as a result of attending this meeting?" The following checklist is a great place to begin.

What is the purpose of your meeting?

____1. To educate your participants about a product, process, or other meaningful content.

____2. To tell others about you or your services.

____3. To have participants achieve a goal such as receiving Continuing Education credit.

____4. To have participants take action on the information they hear such as buying a product or moving a deliverable towards completion.

____5. To share information, feedback, or results with other participants from inside and/or outside your organization.

____6. To have participants come back for more (i.e., go from your free meeting to sign up for paid content or services).

Meetings work best when they are educational and provide value to the participants just for attending the meeting. Points to keep in mind include WIIFM (What's in it for me?) and of course, Principle #1, "People listen for their reasons, not yours."

Are You a Deductive or Inductive Content Creator?

There are two primary approaches for creating content—deductive and inductive. If you are someone who works from a bulleted outline you are a deductive content creator. If you are a brain mapper or someone who enjoys pulling disparate pieces together into a meaningful whole, you are an inductive content creator.

Regardless of your style of content creation, there's an old trainer axiom that applies to almost every type of meeting: "Tell them what you're going to tell them, tell them, and tell them what you told them."

Deductive content creation

If you prefer the outline approach, you are using a deductive approach to create your content. Your style is to start with the big ideas and then fill in the details. Your session will be logical and well-organized.

A major temptation will be to cram your slides full of words. Unfortunately, words on a computer screen are not particularly engaging. In fact, your attendees will quickly read your slides and then tune out just as quickly. Nevertheless, if you're a deductive content creator, starting with a clear outline is the best place for you to begin.

Once you have written your outline, the next step is to search for ways to present as much of your content as possible using photos, graphs, and images rather than using words. In fact, many professional speakers and experienced presenters have shifted to using images with virtually no text. This approach forces attendees to focus on what you are saying rather than scanning the words on their screens and then tuning out.

Inductive content creation

Inductive content creators work from the specific details to the big picture. For leaders who prefer an inductive approach, your challenge will be organizing your material into a logical sequence. Organizing lots of small pieces into a coherent whole is akin to putting together a complicated jigsaw puzzle and can be just as daunting. Here's how to do it.

- Begin by organizing your material using a brain map, digital 3 x 5 cards, or actual 3 x 5 cards.

- Gather all the salient points of your presentation. Place one point on each card.

- Review the information you have written and identify the primary topics you cover.

- Organize cards on the same topic into single stacks.

- Place the cards within each stack so they make sense to you.

- Place a blank card on top of each stack. Read through the cards and write 3-6 words that describe the content in that stack. Those words are the header for that part of your presentation. The remaining cards are the key points you will cover.

- Arrange the stacks in an order that makes sense to you. You now have the outline for your presentation.

Slide Construction 101: How to Engage Your Viewers

Courtesy of video games, action movies, plus numerous other factors, today's meeting participants have short attention spans. This is why it's incredibly important to opt for pictures rather than words as your primary means to engage participants.

To understand why visuals are preferable to words on a page, it's important to understand how physiology influences the processing of incoming information. The Reticular Activating System (RAS) determines the conscious perception of sensory stimuli. It screens out constant background noise such as street traffic, birds singing outside, etc. and is highly attentive to changes in the environment.

Written text and words are processed in the dominant cerebral hemisphere (the left cerebral hemisphere is dominate in 90 percent of the population). In contrast, the non-dominant hemisphere has little ability to process spoken words and virtually no ability to process written words on a screen. What it does do exceptionally well is processing visual imagery instantaneously.

Think back to the last book you read that had pictures. Where did your eyes first go when you turned the page—to the pictures, right? The old saying about a picture being worth a thousand words is true. The right pictures and images can convey your message in a split-second where it might take hundreds of words to achieve the same result.

This is why it's important to keep your session moving with rich visual images to supplement what your participants are hearing. Here are 20 ways to keep your participants highly engaged during your meeting.

Twenty Ways to Make Your Slide Deck More Engaging

(All photos are licensed from Dreamstime.com or Clipart.com.)

1. **Customized or template slides?**
   The first decision you must make is whether you will create a custom template for your slide deck or use a custom design from PowerPoint, Keynote, or from some other provider. If you're presenting for another organization, they often ask you to use their template. If you elect not to use a template, make sure you have a cohesive design. Failure to maintain a consistent format confuses participants and makes you look disorganized.

2. **Tell them what you're going to tell them (learning objectives)**
   Regardless of the type of meeting you're leading, always inform participants about what you will cover first. (Tell them what you're going to tell them.) This makes it easier for participants to focus on key points.

   If you are leading a business meeting, clearly state the purpose of your meeting, the goals you would like to achieve, and any action steps you would like participants to take after the meeting.

   If you are conducting a training or educational session, craft your learning objectives using verbs as in the following slide. If one of your goals is to be hired to speak on your topic, meeting planners usually request that you provide a short summary of your topic plus three actionable takeaways. To write actionable takeaways, use action verbs as illustrated in the next slide.

How to Create a High Impact Presentation

Today you will learn how to:

- Make better choices in terms of how you allocate your time.
- Work less and make more.
- Eliminate energy drainers that block top performance.
- Attract great clients and generate referrals.

3. **White space is your friend**

If you must use a large amount of text on a page, use bullet points and as much white space as possible. Avoid packing in other elements such as photos or animations.

White works the best on virtually all displays. If you want to use a background color, lighter colors with dark print are the easiest to read.

Although some presenters prefer black backgrounds, the backlit nature of computer screens can make these difficult to read. This is especially true if your participants are viewing your slides on a small screen or if your slide contains a large number of bullet points in a small font. If you are going to use a black background, use large fonts as illustrated in the next slide.

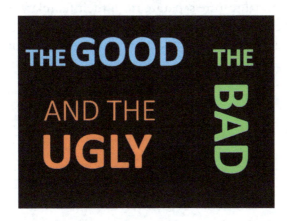

4. **Ask questions**

    While statements do little to engage your brain, questions trigger an active search for an answer. If your question helps participants learn something about themselves, all the better.

    For example, if I asked, "When are you most alert, morning, midday, or evening?" you could ask the question using text. This engages the language portion of the brain and triggers it to search for an answer to the question.

When are you most alert…

Mornings, afternoons, or evenings?

---

5. **Use images and photos whenever possible**

    The previous slide is pretty boring. If you're in a hurry or aren't very good at building creative slides, the more recent versions of Microsoft PowerPoint have a feature called "Design Ideas." This is an additional feature separate from their template solutions.

    For the previous slide, Design Ideas gave me over 30 choices. If the "See More Design Ideas" tab appears, click on it to see additional images. For example:

How to Create a High Impact Presentation

As the following slides illustrate, Design Ideas may also generate an actual photo.

6. Combine a question and photos to help participants learn something about themselves

If you want to use photos, please license them from a reputable site such as Clipart.com, Dreamstime.com, iStock.com, Photos.com, Shutterstock.com, etc. Here's the slide I designed using Dreamstime.com and Clipart.com for a session from my book, *The PQ Factor: Stop Resisting and Start Persisting*.

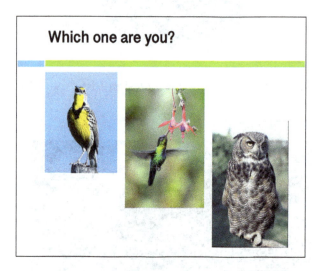

This slide combines a text header with the images of the three birds. The three images engage the visual-processing parts of the brain. The morning lark on the far left represents the early risers, the hummingbird in the middle represents those who are better midday, and the owl represents those are best at night. Since I tend to be a bit of a night owl, I like to add: "See that grumpy-looking owl? That's me when I wake up in the morning."

Participants quickly identify with one of the images. To build interactivity, you could poll the group or use the "hand raise" function to see what percentage of participants are in each group.

These slides also help participants understand how their biorhythms impact their productivity. As a takeaway from this segment, I encourage participants to tackle the most difficult tasks they face each day at the time of day they are most alert.

7. **Use a single photo or image with no text whenever possible**
   The next two slides illustrate how to use a single photo, graphic, or illustration to convey your message without using text. Can you tell what these two slides represent?

   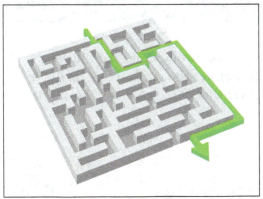

   - The first slide could be used to represent divorce or a child custody dispute.

   - The second slide could be used to convey "out-of-the-box thinking" or finding a "work-around" for a challenging problem.

8. **Use no more than six words per slide whenever possible**
   If you must use words, limit them to six or fewer whenever possible. This keeps you from reading your slides and also keeps the focus on what you're saying. Remember, the audio track is

what matters most. Here are several examples of how to use this approach.

- Place the header or caption over the photo or image you select.

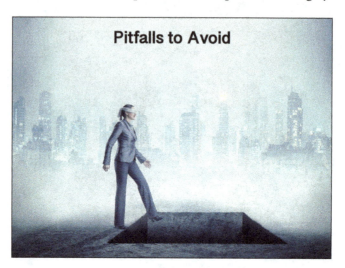

- The following Clipart.com photo had a blank chalkboard. I used the font "Chalkduster" (a standard font on Apple computers), to create this cover slide for a sales training segment on lead conversion.

- Use a "photo object" (an image on a transparent background) and add your text to the white part of the image as illustrated in the following slide.

- You can achieve the same result using a white background and adding an image in portrait mode. Post the image on either side of the screen.

If you're using a template, choose a format where you can post the header or caption at the top or bottom of the slide. The next slide illustrates placing the header at the top. (The meerkat slide illustrated earlier placed the text at the bottom of the slide.)

9. **Header and font size**

    Because users often view sessions on a small screen, it's smart to use larger fonts and fewer words is a smart move. My personal preference is a minimum of a 38-point san serif font for headers and a 28-point sans serif font for the body of my slides. The following slide illustrates these points.

    Create a Negativity Free Mindset
    - Go on a "should" diet.
    - Negative judgments never create positive change.
    - Every piece of negativity you eliminate brings you closer to your goals.

10. **Too many bullet points slay your meeting**

    Leaders who rely predominantly on bullet points almost always end up reading their slides. This is an attention killer because most participants can still read faster than you can talk. This results in disengagement and multi-tasking.

On the other hand, using visuals as often as possible keeps you focused on your connection with your participants. If you only have a few slides with bullet points and you do happen to read them, it's not as much of an issue.

If you must use text, limit the number of bullet points to no more than four points per slide. When possible, use your bullet points as headers to lead into a more in-depth discussion.

11. Avoid listing all your bullet points at once

There are two options for highlighting each point you are making, depending upon the meeting platform you are using.

The first option is to use the custom animation feature in Keynote/PowerPoint to bring up each bullet point as a separate item. (If you're new to presenting, sign up for a training class on how to use PowerPoint or visit one of the Apple tutorials on using Keynote.)

If you are required to submit your slides prior to the meeting so they can be converted into a PDF, any custom animations you included will not work. In other words, the participants will see all the points at once rather than one at a time. You can recreate the same effect by following these simple steps. Assume you have a header and three bullet points:

- On the first slide, delete all points leaving only the header in place.

- On the second slide, delete the last two bullet points, leaving only the first bullet point visible.

- On the third slide, delete the last bullet point.

- The final slide will have the header plus all three bullet points.

Here's what the sequence will look like:

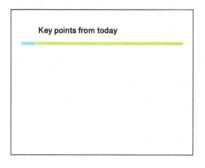 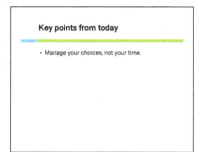

Some presenters prefer to reveal each point separately and delete the other points around it. Our recommendation is to avoid doing so because it creates visual confusion. The display mimics how people normally read slides and how the session would appear to participants if the animation feature was available.

12. Screen layout when you have people or animals in the photo

If you use a photo with people or animals, make sure the people are looking directly at the viewer whenever possible.

13. More slides = more engagement

Having a large number of slides in a face-to-face presentation can be highly distracting (it places the emphasis on your slide deck rather than your connection to the audience), the exact opposite is true on virtual meetings. The reason becomes apparent when you consider how people browse the web. Unless something grabs their attention, they generally surf from image-to-image and site-to-site.

I personally prefer a rate of about one slide per minute for face-to-face meetings. If you're using a platform such as Zoom where you and the slides are visible next to your video feed, one slide per minute is also about the right pace depending upon your rate of speech. If you're using slides only (no video), pick up the pace to about 2-4 slides per minute depending upon the nature of the content.

14. Too much animation can slay your meeting as well

If you are an inductive content creator, the temptation may be to include too many visuals. Having lots of flying and twirling visual effects distracts your participants' attention from what you are saying. Again, this is due to the RAS which is highly tuned to changes in the environment. Remember, less is more.

Also keep in mind that while your animated content may look great on your computer, it can be an entirely different experience for participants with slow connections. In fact, if the animation you're using requires a large amount of bandwidth, buffering can result. This can cause the participant's computer to lock up or disconnect. When this happens, many won't bother to log back on your meeting.

15. Use quizzes to build engagement

Quizzes are a powerful way to increase engagement on any virtual meeting, whether it's live or a replay. Here are three slides I use to train participants why they should never use unlicensed photos on their website, presentations, or anywhere else. In this segment, I describe what happened to our company when a designer used a copyrighted Getty image from Google Images without obtaining the appropriate licensing agreement. Making matters worse, he didn't advise us about what he had done.

I begin the segment with a question, followed by a multiple-choice quiz.

How much would you pay to post this picture on your website?

- $25.00
- $50.00
- $275.00
- $650.00
- $1,300.00

I then explain this **IMPORTANT CAVEAT:**

Avoid using Google Images because many of these are licensed from third party providers. This means the site posting these images paid a licensing fee to do so. If you use the photos without paying the licensing fee, you run the chance of being charged with copyright infringement, which can literally cost you thousands of dollars.

At that point I display the next slide which answers the question:

> **How much would you pay to post this picture on your website?**
>
> - $25.00
> - $50.00
> - $275.00
> - $650.00
> - **$1,300.00**

I follow up by sharing what happened regarding this issue.

Getty images sent us a bill for $1,300. When we checked with our Intellectual Property attorney, he said even though we didn't post the picture ourselves, the person we hired did. We had no choice but to pay the demand letter. I did negotiate the charge down to $650.00. Even so, it was a very expensive lesson.

To make sure this doesn't happen to you, use a photo licensing site. Whenever possible, avoid using clipart images. Use photos and high-quality graphics to make your point instead.

16. Charts, spreadsheets, and other detailed visuals

The challenge with charts, spreadsheets, and other visuals with small print is the text is too small for easy reading. A chart using a bar graph or some other easily understood graphic is a plus. For example, rather than giving participants a lot of numbers and words describing what those numbers mean, a line or bar graph can summarize the data in an easy-to-digest format.

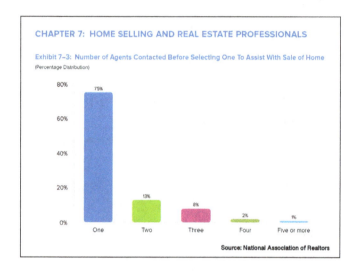

As a rule of thumb, avoid using any graphic that has small print unless there is no other viable option. A different approach is to display the key points one at a time in separate slides.

17. Using "symbols"

Arrows, boxes, and other symbols provide a powerful means to combine text with a graphic. The following two slides show how to direct the viewer's attention to the key point on each slide even though the slide is packed with numbers and text.

Interest Rates and The Cost of Waiting to Purchase
$200,000 loan (numbers rounded to the nearest whole dollar)

Interest Rate	Mo. Pay	Mo cost for increase	Annual cost increase	30-year cost 1% increase	30-yr cost for 2% increase
4% to 5%	$955 $1,074	$119 (1%)	$1,428	$42,772 ←	
5% to 6%	$1,074 $1,199	$125 (1%)	$1,500	$45,165	
4% to 6%	$955 $1,199	$244 (2%)	$2,928 (2%) increase		$87,937 (4% to 6%)

Interest Rates and The Cost of Waiting to Purchase
$200,000 loan (numbers rounded to the nearest whole dollar)

Interest Rate	Mo. Pay	Mo cost for increase	Annual cost increase	30-year cost 1% increase	30-yr cost for 2% increase
4% to 5%	$955 $1,074	$119 (1%)	$1,428	$42,772	
5% to 6%	$1,074 $1,199	$125 (1%)	$1,500	$45,165	↓
4% to 6%	$955 $1,199	$244 (2%)	$2,928 (2%) increase		$87,937 (4% to 6%)

18. Look for relationships

As you prepare your slide deck, constantly search for relationships. Examples include timelines, processes, cause and effect, multiple options leading to a single outcome, etc. The next slide uses PowerPoint's "Smart Art" to illustrate how many listings Realtors lose each year if they fail to stay in contact with their sphere of influence.

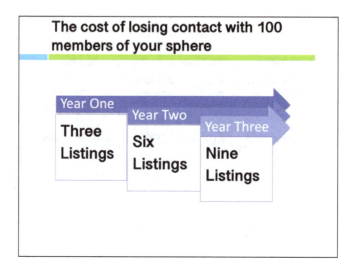

19. Use verbs rather than adjectives

To keep engagement high, use verbs rather than adjectives. If you look at most sales copy, it's usually devoted to describing all the features of the product. Descriptions relying on adjectives usually fail to engage the brain. For example, if you say, "Really lovely pool," all the brain hears is the word "Pool."

Now compare this statement: "Dive into the sparkling pool and unwind with a relaxing swim at the end of a long day." The verbs help the brain create an engaging picture about how good this would feel. Consequently, when you can't use an image, focus on using action verbs rather than adjectives.

20. Videos increase engagement

Usually it's wise to have some sort of participant engagement every 7-10 minutes. In addition to the other ideas we discussed, videos are one of the best ways to break up the content while also increasing engagement. This is especially true if you use a funny video.

Three important points to note:

- If you're using a HD camera to shoot video, your file sizes will often be over one gigabyte unless you compress the file. Even with compression, however, video files can take a long period of time to upload from your computer and can take even longer to download to your participants' computers. An alternative is to shoot the video in HD but save it at a lower resolution.

- Never try to stream a video live if you're broadcasting live to your participants. In other words, if you're delivering a live virtual meeting, embed your videos in your slides rather than trying to play them from the web. This will avoid a wide variety of problems, especially those having to do with bandwidth. This also applies to face-to-face presentations. Your slide deck needs to stand alone without connecting to the web.

- Please Note: like copyrighted images, if you pull videos from online, contact the creator to request permission to use the video. For a more complete discussion, search "YouTube videos and fair use." The safest thing to do is to shoot your own videos.

Chapter 7 Key Points

1. While face-to-face meetings rely primarily on visual cues, in all virtual meetings the auditory is primary.

2. As you plan your virtual meeting, it's important to identify the type of meeting you will be leading, which in turn determines the type of content to include. The four primary meeting types are:
    - Education or training.
    - Influence.
    - Inspire.
    - Sell.

3. Determine whether you are a deductive or inductive content creator and follow the suggested guidelines appropriate to your content creation style.

4. Whenever possible, use photos, images, and videos rather than text.

5. Minimize the number of words on any slide (no more than 3-4 bullet points per page) and select easy-to-read font sizes that will be sharp and clear on both small and large screens.

6. Avoid using images you find online, even if a site claims to have "free photos." Protect yourself by using one of the photo licensing sites such as Dreamstime.com or Clipart.com. The penalties for using a single unlicensed photo can be a $1,000 or more per image.

7. Videos are a powerful way to increase visual engagement. Take your own videos or use a licensing site to avoid copyright issues.

You have identified your topic and have over 20 different ways to make your meeting more engaging visually. The next step is to determine how you can deliver the auditory portion of your content as effectively as possible.

Chapter 8:
Improve Your Delivery

*Public speaking is the number-one
fear... even over death!*
Emily Deschanel

You have put together your checklists, determined which platform you will use, and prepared your slides. In addition to the strategies and techniques discussed in the previous chapters, what other steps can you take to improve the delivery of your meeting content?

Interactive Video or Webinar?

When you select your delivery platform, carefully consider what format will be best for you and your participants. For example, if you're delivering a content-rich webinar, training class, or online education for a large group, a webinar platform where only your slides and your video feed are visible is a great choice. These platforms are specifically designed to handle large meetings. They are also less likely to have bandwidth issues because they're not receiving a continuous video feed from participants.

On the other hand, drawbacks include decreased opportunity for interaction with participants. Furthermore, keeping your energy high and building engagement is much more challenging when your only point of interaction is the little dot where your camera is located. This is especially true for anyone who is accustomed to leading face-to-face.

Start Strong and End Strong

When you're presenting face-to-face, especially if you're delivering a keynote, most experts agree you should start strong and end strong. Engage your audience with a compelling story or some other attention-grabbing content. As you begin your closing sequence, especially if you're delivering a keynote, pick up your pace, your level of excitement, and deliver a "Wow" moment to wrap up the session.

Virtual meetings are different. If the length of your meeting is more than 5-10 minutes, divide your content into chunks of about 5-7 minutes. Create engagement right from the start of each segment with a quiz, poll, story, or funny video. This approach re-engages participants whose attention may have been diverted elsewhere. Changing your rate of speech, your tone of voice, or inflection can also re-engage their attention.

How Fast Do You Speak?

While the human brain can think up to 1,000 words per minute, most professional speakers speak at a rate of about 160 words per minute. To make sure your delivery is as effective as possible, begin by determining how fast you speak. Here's what to do:

- Copy and paste an article into your word processor.

- Set a timer for exactly one minute and read the article out loud.

- Once the timer goes off, mark where you were. Use your mouse to highlight those words in your word processor.

- Use the "word count" feature on your word processor to determine how many words you read. That's your rate of speech.

- Repeat the process to confirm the first number was correct.

- Should you use a teleprompter? Teleprompters can train you to speak at a consistent rate of about 160 words per minute. In terms of relying on using a teleprompter during your actual meeting, don't do it! This produces the same effect as reading from your slides—it breaks your connection and reduces engagement. Rely on your talking points instead.

Visual, Auditory, or Kinesthetic—How Is Your Brain Wired?

Did you know your rate of speech is influenced by how your brain is wired for learning? About 40 percent of the population learns best visually, another 40 percent learn best auditorily, and the remaining 20 percent learn best kinesthetically (through what they feel or touch).

- **Visual learners**
  Those who learn best visually are usually fast talkers, especially when they become nervous. They're also more likely to be concerned with how they look on video-based meetings as well as with the appearance of their background.

  If you are visual and speak at a rate of 170 words per minute or more, practice slowing down your rate of speech. If you fail to do so, your kinesthetic participants will struggle to follow what you're saying. This is why relying more on visuals with no more than six words whenever possible is so important. Both visuals and kinesthetics can grasp a concept more easily when it's presented pictorially rather than in words.

- **Auditory learners**
  People who are auditory learn best by what they hear. Anyone who has a "radio voice," who is an accomplished musician, or is good at telling great stories is usually an auditory learner. If you are auditory learner, you were born to lead great audio-only meetings. You quickly comprehend what's spoken as opposed to those who are visual and kinesthetic who process auditory information less efficiently. Your voice and pace are usually easy for most people to follow. You're especially effective when telling a story that brings what you're covering to life.

  This is one trait the very best keynote speakers share—they seldom work with a slide deck. Instead, they rely on their voice and their body language to inspire and motivate their audiences. Kinesthetics respond to the feelings the auditory leader elicits, making it easier for them to connect with kinesthetic participants as well.

If you're auditory, the thought of constructing a slide deck packed with lots of words and visuals probably makes your stomach churn. If it's really necessary to create a detailed slide deck, you can use a transcription tool such as Otter.ai to capture what you want to say. You can also record directly into Otter live. If you have an MP3 or MP4 file from previous meetings, Otter can create a written transcript for those as well.

Once you have the transcript, it's easy to find someone who can create a slide deck with the words and visuals required to support your participants who are visual learners. (Upwork.com is a great source.)

- **Kinesthetic learners**
 If you're someone who learns best by doing or having hands-on experience, you are a kinesthetic learner. Virtual meetings are probably not your strong suit. One of my nieces is a kinesthetic learner. Even though she was on the Dean's List, she struggled with her online classes. Where she really excelled was in the labs and other classes that provided hands-on experience.

 If you are kinesthetic, you are more concerned about feeling comfortable as opposed to how you look. In fact, you may have shown up for past virtual meetings in your pajamas or looking disheveled. Kinesthetic learners often speak more slowly than those who are visual or auditory. If your pace is 150 words per minute or less, you need to pick it up. Otherwise, your slow rate of speech can cause your auditory and visual participants to tune out.

Use Your Voice to Manage the Room

Do you want to sound more powerful when you speak? Regardless of the type of virtual meeting you are leading, the secret to sounding powerful when you speak is to use "downstrokes." To understand how this works, say the following sentence out loud. "It's raining outside."

Did you notice how your voice naturally dropped at the end of the sentence? Also, when you say, "Good morning," "Good afternoon," and "Good evening" out loud, you will notice your voice naturally drops in a downstroke. The same is true when you say, "Goodbye."

On the other hand, if you regularly speak in upstrokes, you sound tentative and weak. Say the word "Hello" out loud.

The word "Hello" is typically spoken with an upstroke. Notice the difference from the three greetings vs. saying "Hello."

Powerful speakers end their sentences in downstrokes, as do most men. When girls are growing up, however, they're taught to speak in upstrokes. This is the reason women can sound tentative or indecisive when they speak. In fact, when Hollywood wants to make a woman sound stupid, they typically give her blond hair, a high-pitched voice, and have her speak in sentences ending with an upstroke.

The next script is from my training on how real estate agents can invite neighbors to an open house for their new listing. Read the script out loud before going to the next paragraph. Pay special attention to how you ask the question in the last sentence.

Mr. and Mrs. Seller have asked me to personally invite you to our open house on Sunday from 1:00-3:00 p.m. at 123 Main Street. We're serving refreshments. Will you be able to attend?

If you're like most people, you ended the first two sentences of the script with a downstroke. In terms of the final sentence, the word "attend" ends in a downstroke. When English speakers ask a question, however, they use an upstroke at the end of sentence. So, did you use an upstroke or a downstroke when you asked, "Will you be able to attend?"

If you said, "attend" with an upstroke, try repeating the sentence and saying "attend" with a downstroke. Can you hear how "attend" said with a downstroke sounds more persuasive than when you say it with an upstroke?

As a virtual meeting leader, using downstrokes makes you sound more confident, helps you make your points more effectively, and also helps you to handle distractions and challenges more easily.

Avoid the Following Words that Weaken Your Delivery

When you engage with your participants live, the following six words can make you sound weak, indecisive, and unsure of yourself. Here's what to do to sound stronger and more confident as you interact with your participants. (By the way, if you are in a negotiation, avoiding these words will allow you to be a more powerful negotiator as well.)

1. **But**

   Even if you have heard this before, it bears repeating here. "But" negates whatever comes before it. For example, "I want to lead great virtual meetings, but I'm not very good on video."

   A simple way to avoid "but" is to substitute the word "and." "I want to lead great virtual meetings and I'm not very good on video."

   In the first example, "but" negates the statement, "I want to lead great virtual meetings." In other words, it says you do NOT want to lead great virtual meetings. In the second example, using "and" avoids negating the first statement.

2. **Can't**

   "Can't" is ambiguous. For example, when a real estate agent says, "I can't go door knocking," do they mean, "I am physically unable to go door knocking," "It is illegal in my area to go door knocking," or "I don't want to go door-knocking"?

   When most people use "can't," they're really saying, "I choose not to engage in this behavior." They often use "can't" to cover up their real intention.

   Consequently, whenever possible, substitute the word "choose" for the word "can't." "Choose" puts you in power; "can't" takes your power away.

   Henry Ford summed this up best when he said, "Whether you think you can, or you think you can't—you're right."

   The bottom line is if you believe you can lead effective virtual meetings, the probability is high you will learn to do so. On the other hand, if you expect to have a raft of problems, are constantly frustrated by the technology, and continually grumble about the challenges in leading virtual meetings, as Henry Ford observed, "you're right."

3. **"Hope" and "If"**

   The words "hope" and "if" make you sound weak. In terms of using the word "hope," substitute the word "can."

"I hope I can learn to lead effective virtual meetings," vs. "I can (am able to) lead effective virtual meetings."

For the word "if," substitute the word "when."

"If I can learn to lead effective virtual meetings," vs. "When I learn to lead effective virtual meetings."

While these differences are subtle, the difference is that of confidence vs. uncertainty.

4. **Not**

Whenever possible, avoid using the word "not." This includes contractions such as "can't" and "won't." The reason for doing is based upon how your brain processes incoming verbal information in "Broca's Area 10." This structure is part of the Reticular Activating System (RAS) which determines what is admitted into your conscious thoughts. Neuroscientists have nicknamed Broca's Area 10 "Mother."

The problem is "Mother" can only process one thought at a time. For example, if you say, "I don't want to get sick," your brain processes that statement in two separate steps, just as a computer program would. "Mother" must first process the statement without the word "not." In other words, what you're telling your brain is, "I want to get sick." Then it processes the word, "not."

This is a great tip for both you as a leader as well as your participants. Avoid any sentence, phrase, or contraction that includes the word "not." Using the previous example, you would say, "I want to avoid becoming sick." In most cases, substituting the word "avoid" for "not," eliminates the issue.

5. **Should**

Have you ever noticed how often people use the word "should?" Rather than listening to what matters most to the other person, most people use the word "should" as a strategy to get what they want. We also use "should" as a way to make ourselves feel guilty about our choices, e.g., "I should go on a diet."

To see how prevalent "should" is in your life, go on a "should" diet for a week. Notice how you and others use "should." In most cases, the manipulation ploy is obvious. Once you realize this, do your best to strike "should" from your vocabulary.

6. **Try**

People use the word "try" when they're uncertain as to whether they can do something. For example, if you tell someone, "I'll try to be there," you're really saying you may not be able to be there. The challenge with "try" is the other person usually hears, "I'll be there."

For you as the leader, be definite. Instead of saying, "I'll try to get the handout to you no later than tomorrow," say what you can definitely do. "The handout will be sent to you via email no later than 5:00 tomorrow afternoon. If you haven't received it by then, please email me so I can make sure you receive it.

If one of your participants uses "try," especially if this is work related or something required for a team to complete a project, be direct. Ask, "At what time can you definitely commit to having this work completed?"

Control Your Body Language

One of the simplest and yet most difficult things to control when you are leading video-based virtual meetings is your body language. Even if you are well-prepared and have great content, it's difficult to keep from fidgeting in your chair for a full 30-60 minutes while still maintaining eye contact. Remember Principle #6, "What you do is what you will get." If you are fidgety or nervous, your participants will fidget right along with you. Here's what to do to control your body language in order to obtain the best possible results from your virtual meeting.

- Use a straight-back chair. As much as I love my custom office chair, using a straight back with no wheels helps me keep my body language still.

- Always check your video settings to determine if your video feed matches what you are seeing on your monitor as you record. In the next screen shot, my podcast guest and I were both looking

Improve Your Delivery

at each other on our monitors but looking in the wrong direction on the recording.

The simplest way to correct this situation is to focus your eyes slightly below where your camera is situated and then record. If you are not looking directly back at the person who will be viewing your video, experiment until you find exactly where to focus.

Record Yourself

The most accurate way to see how you will look and sound to your participants is to rehearse on the computer you will use for your meeting. When you practice delivering your content, be sure you set the platform you use to record both audio-only (MP3) and the full video (MP4). As you can see, Zoom gives you the option of not only accessing the video and the audio separately, you can also obtain the audio-only for each speaker. Personally, I love this option because first, it makes it easier for my video editor to clean up issues with the sound on a single track and second, it allows me to repurpose the video meeting content for our audio-only podcasts.

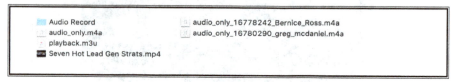

Here's how to evaluate what you recorded.

- Begin by evaluating what you did well. This is essential because your goal in applying The Six Principle Model is to build on your strengths.

- Next, playback the MP3 track first to see what you sound like to anyone who is unable to access the meeting using the video.

- Be honest—was your pace too slow or too fast? If you're speaking at 170 words per minute or more, practice slowing down. If you're speaking at 150 words per minute or less, practice speeding it up.

- Listen for "uhs" and other fillers. (One of my personal favorites is "so" as a transition word to start a new section of content.)

- Listen for the words discussed in the previous section that weaken your delivery. Which ones did you use and how often? You will be more likely to use these words when you are interacting with participants as opposed to when you're doing a straight content delivery.

- Once you identify a filler, word, or other phrase you are overusing, ask a friend or family member to say the word, "Pause," every time you use the phrase you are attempting to eliminate.

Awareness is the first step in reducing how many times you use these words.

- Repeat the process by playing back the MP4 recording to see how you look while leading.

- Did you look directly at your participants as if you were speaking to them in a conversation or were you looking elsewhere?

- Evaluate your body language. Do you look comfortable? Were you bobbing around in your chair or fidgeting? Your goal is to eliminate as many of the distracting movements as possible and stay in a conversational mode with your participants.

- When you rehearse, note where the natural pauses exist in your presentation. These can be the times to handoff to a co-presenter, to take questions, or to ask for participant feedback.

- A word of caution: If the people around you use poor speech patterns, you can easily pick up their speech patterns, especially if it is someone with whom you spend a lot of time.

- Practice, practice, practice.

While this may be painful, stay focused on the changes you can make to improve the participant experience. By the way, EVERYONE hates how they look and sound when they first start recording themselves, whether it's on audio-only or video. You WILL get used to it!

Chapter 8 Key Points

1. Because the auditory on any virtual meeting is always primary, it's especially important to devote time to evaluating how you come across on the audio. Again, if there are bandwidth issues or other reasons you or your participants are unable to access the video feed, you must always be prepared to lead an auditory-only meeting.

2. Make your audio more engaging by changing your rate of speech, your tone of voice, and your inflection.

3. Vary your content to fit the needs of all types of learners, i.e., visual, auditory, and kinesthetic.

4. Strive to maintain a speaking rate of about 160 words per minute. Record yourself and listen to how you sound. You can use a teleprompter to practice for speed but avoid using it during your actual meeting.

5. Using "downstrokes" when you speak makes you sound confident and in control. Speaking in upstrokes makes you sound tentative and weak.

6. Keep your body language as "quiet" as possible when you're leading to avoid detracting from the audio feed. Using a straight back chair can be helpful.

7. Review the "Words to Avoid" list. A great way to train yourself to avoid using them is to practice in normal conversation rather than when you're leading. Practice does work!

Chapter 9:
Meeting Day: Fifteen Common Mistakes to Avoid

When you make a mistake, there are only three things you should ever do about it: admit it, learn from it, and don't repeat it.
Coach Paul "Bear" Bryant

You have identified the tools and systems you will use, written your agenda/presentation, and created your supporting materials. What other steps can you take to make your meeting as effective as possible?

The following list contains 15 of the most common mistakes virtual meeting leaders make. If you currently engage in any of these behaviors, eliminate them as soon as possible. If you're new to leading virtual meetings, employing the following best practices will help you to avoid the pitfalls that can undermine your success.

Common Mistake #1: Failure to Systematize How You Handle Logistics

Regardless of your experience level, systematization increases your effectiveness. The checklists in this book will help you to systematize the many details virtual meetings require. Handling these issues at the onset allows you to focus on your leadership and increasing participant engagement. This is especially important if you are leading on a platform you haven't used before.

Some examples of checklists found in Chapter 6 include:

- The tools and systems you will need

- Logistics

- Presenters and their roles

- Selecting a strong topic

- Your presentation style

Use these checklists as a starting point and make alterations as your experience grows.

Common Mistake #2: Failure to Review Your Slide Deck the Evening Before and the Day of Your Meeting

Review your slide deck before you go to sleep the night before your presentation. This anchors the material more thoroughly in your brain. It's also smart to do a second review the day of your meeting. If you're prone to pre-meeting nerves, reviewing the content twice reduces any anxiety you may be experiencing.

Common Mistake #3: Failure to Send Out "Guidelines for Participants"

Make sure your participants receive your meeting guidelines prior to the meeting. Here's what to include:

1. How to log into the meeting.

2. The phone numbers to call if they're joining the meeting by phone and whom to contact if they have trouble logging on to the meeting.

3. For those who are dialing into the meeting, instructions on how to mute their audio if they're using their computer or mobile device. (Many platforms allow you to mute everyone when they first arrive to your meeting or class. If you want to call on a participant you can unmute them individually.)

4. Control background noise by using "Mute all participants" or "global mute." If this is not an option, most platforms allow participants to mute their audio feed. Alternatively, there's a mute button on almost every desktop phone and mobile device—ask all participants to use it.

5. If you're leading on a video conferencing platform such as Microsoft Teams, Skype, or Zoom, instructions for turning off their video feed in case there is a bandwidth issue that is causing both the audio and the video to break up. Remember, the audio feed is the most important part of your meeting or class.

As mentioned in Chapter 5, for auditory-only meetings remind participants to "Say your name first," whenever they speak. Introduce this concept at the beginning of your meeting as well as reminding participants who forget to do so during the meeting.

Common Mistake #4: Arriving Less Than 30 Minutes Before the Start Time

Whenever you lead a class, webinar, or other large meeting where you are working with a slide deck, arrive 30 minutes early as we discussed before. This gives you time to troubleshoot glitches before starting the meeting. This is especially important if you're leading on another organization's platform. Even if you're familiar with leading meetings on the same platform the organization is using, the platform can behave quite differently based upon the host's version of the software, their operating system, as well as how they set up their preferences.

Microsoft's PowerPoint program is a prime example. If you are designing slides using the latest version of Microsoft 365 on your PC and your host is using the latest Mac version (or vice versa), any custom template you created, special formatting, or other special effects often look very different on the host's platform. This problem increases exponentially if you or your host are using older versions of PowerPoint or if you are using a personal version and the other party is using an enterprise version.

If you arrive 30 minutes early as we suggest, you have time to quickly run through your slides and correct issues on the run. You can avoid this issue by having the host pre-load your slides or doing a dry run prior to your live meeting. A different alternative is to save your slide deck to a PDF file, but this takes up a great deal of bandwidth. Also, PDF files are often blurrier than your original slide deck.

Common Mistake #5: "Waiting for Organizer"

Have you ever attended a virtual meeting where you logged in exactly on time and were greeted with a screen that says, "Waiting for Organizer"? An even worse situation occurs when the leader logs in, the screen is blank, and there's nothing but dead silence.

Your opportunity to engage your participants begins the moment the first participant arrives. A simple way to do this is to have a conversation between the presenters/moderators a little bit before the scheduled start time. This allows early birds to become immediately engaged in your topic. It also allows you to welcome people as they log on.

Some webinar platforms have a function called "practice mode" that allows you to interact with participants. You can use this feature to chat with your participants prior to starting the regular meeting. When you're ready to begin the meeting, you will switch to presentation mode and place all participants on global mute.

Most platforms allow you to individually unmute a single participant. This allows participants to ask questions directly rather than only using the chat. You can also use the "raise hand function" to call on people, however, the chat lets you choose the questions you feel are most relevant. When people raise their hand, it's like it is in any classroom situation. The question may be irrelevant or something you would prefer to answer after covering your core agenda or content.

By the same token, you can ask the group questions. The "raise hand" feature works particularly well in this scenario to "surface the wisdom of the group."

Common Mistake #6: Not Attending to the Housekeeping First

Before turning the session over to the presenter, the moderator covers housekeeping items. These include how to log back on if someone gets disconnected from the meeting, whether the speaker will take questions during the session or hold them until the end, plus the phone number for technical or other types of issues.

Here's an example of what to say:

Welcome to our webinar on "How to Lead Effective Virtual Meetings." To make sure we answer as many of your questions as possible, there will be 15 minutes of Q&A at the end of today's meeting. Post any questions you may have in the chat. I (the moderator or you as the leader) will answer as many of them as possible. If we don't have enough time to cover all the questions or if you need additional information, please email me at Leader@MyOrganization.com. I'll be happy to answer your questions offline.

This best practice invites participants to interact by asking questions and gives them a way to have their questions answered after the meeting.

If you're leading a group of more than 20, it's smart to have a moderator who handles the housekeeping, monitors questions, and handles any other issues. The challenge with leading solo is whatever is happening on the chat can easily become a distraction. Having a moderator allows you to maximize your connection with the group, keeps the meeting moving forward, and keeps you from being derailed by non-relevant comments or questions.

Common Mistake #7: Not Providing Your Supporting Materials Prior to the Meeting

Always send out your meeting agenda, handouts, or any other supporting materials prior to the meeting. As I mentioned earlier, when my internet went out during a webinar for over 1,400 people, I was able to continue the webinar by phone because everyone had the handout.

If you're concerned your participants will skip the live meeting if you provide the content, post a link in the chat where participants can download whatever documents you want to share at the beginning of the meeting and midway through the meeting for any late arrivers. Alternatively, you can email participants the complete notes after the session or you can post the slides on your website, Slideshare.com, SlideServe.com, or SpeakerDeck.com.

Common Mistake #8: Long Intros

While your intro must be about you, keep it short—no more than 150 words (about one minute). If someone else is introducing you, give them a written script. As mentioned earlier, long introductions are both attention and attendance killers. This comes back to Principle #1: "People listen for their reasons, not yours."

Common Mistake #9: Not Telling Them What You're Going to Tell Them

This tip comes the master of rhetoric himself, Aristotle:

Tell them what you are going to tell them, tell them, then tell them what you told them.

In other words, at the beginning of your session, cover the highlights from your meeting agenda or if you're conducting a class or training, your 3-5 most important learning objectives for the session. Once you have delivered your content, review the key points again at the end of the meeting.

Common Mistake #10: The "Content Download"

If you ever feel compelled to talk for the entire length of your meeting, conduct a trial run of your upcoming meeting and record it on your computer or Zoom. No matter how painful it is, play the entire recording back. Then, the next time you're tempted to do a content download, replay the recording to remind yourself how important it is to break up the content with interactivity.

Common Mistake #11: Believing You Cannot Create Interactivity During Asynchronous Meetings and Classes

As a rule of thumb, include some sort of break in the content every 5-7 minutes. There are numerous ways to do this.

- **Conduct a poll**
  This is excellent way to not only provide a break in the content, but to also build interactivity.

- **Use a multiple-choice quiz**
  If your meeting is being recorded for individual replay, polling is not an option. You can still use a multiple-choice quiz. For example, in my course on digital marketing I might ask,

  Which of the following has the highest open rate?

  a. Videos

  b. Pictures

  c. Email

  d. Voicemail

After displaying the quiz question and highlighting the correct answer in the next slide ("videos"), I provide the research with the open rates for each option.

- **Ask a question that helps them learn something about themselves**
  Even if you are pre-recording a class for individual replay, this technique still works extremely well. For example, when I train on how to improve your life by ridding yourself of "tolerations" (the little and big annoyances that can pull you off focus), I generally ask the participants to do the following:

  > *Please write down five things that are bugging you right now. It could be a dripping faucet in the bathroom, the button that popped off your favorite shirt, or something as serious as leaving your job or relationship.*

  I then pause for 60-90 seconds while they create their list. If you are doing this session live, ask participants to post some of their more unusual or fun tolerations in the chat. Whether or not you take shares, be prepared with your own examples illustrating this concept.

- **Rather than just talking about the point you want to make, share a photo illustrating the point instead**
  If your organization is entering a Halloween decorating contest, rather than having participants describe their ideas verbally, challenge them to find the oddest or most unusual photos they can locate and share them with the group. This taps into Principle #2, "People support what they help to create," and Principle #4: "Surface the wisdom of the group." (The photos in the next slides are from Dreamstime.com.)

- **Make them laugh**
  Using the Halloween example, you could kick it up a notch by sharing something funny or over the top. (Search for "crazy pumpkin scarecrows" online for some ideas.) Laughter increases beta endorphins, the "feel good" neurotransmitter

Meeting Day: Fifteen Common Mistakes to Avoid

that also strengthens immunity. When you make them laugh, that good feeling is attached to you.

- **Engage your participants with short topical videos**
I often reference Dr. Paul Pearsall's research in my training. Pearsall uncovered some surprising factors that contribute to heart disease as well as key steps to avoid it. The most important factor to avoid all types of serious illness is laughing 100 times per day.

  Rather than explaining this factor first, I lead into the segment by saying, "Here's the most important step you can take to avoid heart disease." I then play a video of a dad sitting making funny noises and shaking his head back and forth while his baby quadruplets laugh uncontrollably.

As a rule of thumb, the shorter the video the better. Short videos can be excellent lead-ins to the next portion of the content as well as transitions between topics. Remember, video is one of the best ways to engage your participants and inject fun into your session.

Common Mistake #12: It's All About Me!

There's an old sales adage called WIIFM—"What's in it for me?" The following illustrates a leader who is "me-focused" rather than "participant-focused."

> *I thought you would enjoy hearing a little bit about who I am and what I've done. When I was in high school, I played the guitar in a rock and roll band and traveled all over the country doing gigs. That's where I figured out how much my musical background can help you with your personal and business relationships. By the way, I now have three kids. Here's a picture of me and my family. Aren't my girls beautiful? I'm teaching them all how to play the guitar too!*

The speaker in the example references "I," "me," or "my" 13 times. This "me-me-me" approach doesn't work well for any type of meeting.

A simple way to eliminate this problem is to replace "I" language with "you" language. Here's an example of a "you-focused" approach on the same topic:

> *Have you ever considered how your taste in music might reveal something important about who you are as person? Daniel Levitin, a neuroscientist at McGill University and the author of "This Is Your Brain on Music," is also a musician. He believes musical taste falls into five categories. Which of the following five types of music do you like best?*

The previous example uses "you" language to engage the participants. The speaker then has the option of using any of the four following techniques to create additional interactivity.

1. Play sample clips of music representing each of the five types.

2. Conduct a poll to determine how many people prefer each type. The speaker or moderator reports the results.

3. The leader shares what the research says about the people who prefer each type of music. The leader then polls how many participants agree with what the research says about their preference in music.

4. To wrap up this segment, the leader could share a powerful takeaway (a "WIIFM" statement) about what this means for the participants' relationships. For example:

   This may be why people seek romantic partners with similar musical tastes. It's not small talk. You're communicating really important information about yourself—what your core beliefs are.

The previous example draws from the following facts:

- People love taking quick quizzes or polls that help them learn something about themselves. Having them respond to the poll or "raise their hand" builds interactivity.

- Asking questions also shifts the participant's focus from receiving information to formulating what they would do in a specific situation.

- Adding the musical content allows the participant's brain to shift from being focused in their dominant cerebral hemisphere where language is processed (usually the "left brain" in most people) to the cerebral hemisphere (usually the "right brain") that processes emotion and non-verbal content.

- Using expert research is more persuasive than giving your opinion.

Common Mistake #13: Reading the Slides to Your Participants

Your participants can read faster than you talk. Reading your slides is a sure way to have your participants disengage. As noted in Chapter 7, a better approach is to select a photo, an illustration, graph, or some other type of image to illustrate the point without using words. This approach engages both sides of the brain while driving home the point both visually and auditorily.

Common Mistake #14: Packing Too Much Content on a Single Slide

As outlined in Chapter 7, if you have a header and more than four bullet points on a single slide, you have too much content. Just to review, if you must use bullet points, make them as brief as possible. For headers, use a minimum of a 38-40-point font and 28-32-point font for bullet points. Limit the number of points to four per page. Having plenty of white space makes your slides easier to read.

If a picture is worth a thousand words, the takeaway is never use text if an image or photo alone will do the job. Remember, less is more.

CAVEAT:

Although we mentioned this earlier, it still bears repeating, take your own photos or use a paid service such as Clipart.com, Dreamstime.com, or iStockphoto.com for your photos, web graphics, animations, etc. The two sites I use most often are Clipart.com and Dreamstime.com given the millions of images and photos they provide and their competitive pricing.

Never use any image you find online unless you have a license to use it!

Common Mistake #15: Not Ending on Time

There are three components to this issue. The first is the time component itself. People are busy and if you're scheduled for one hour, that's how much time they have allotted.

Second, failure to provide all the content you committed to cover in the time allotted means you over promised and under delivered. This in turn can result in participants feeling disappointed, frustrated, or even angry which undermines the goals you set for your meeting.

This is another reason it's important to supply supporting materials to your participants. You're much less likely to have a problem if you fail to cover all the material.

Third, if you promise 10 or 15 minutes of Q&A and you still haven't covered all the items you intended to cover, participants usually prefer to forego the Q&A in favor of covering the key content. If you still have key content you haven't covered during the allotted time, you can be available after the meeting to answer any questions they may have. Alternatively, you can share your slides or post a link where they can download the content they missed.

Chapter 9 Key Points

1. Checklists are the foundation for building systems, especially at the beginning of your meeting. Customize the checklists from Chapter 6 to fit the type of meeting you are leading. The more systematized you can make your meetings, the more time you can devote to delivering engaging content and creating interactivity.

2. Always review your slides, send out "Guidelines for Participants," plus any supporting materials (e.g. an agenda or handout) prior to your meeting.

3. Avoid content downloads, keep your slides simple, and never use text when an image or picture does a better job.

4. Arrive early, start on time, end on time, and handle any housekeeping details at the beginning of your meeting.

5. Avoid long intros, content downloads, and reading your slides to participants. Be "participant-focused," not "me-focused."

6. Use polling, quizzes, funny photos, and topical videos to increase engagement, especially in asynchronous meetings.

7. Select at least two of the ideas from this chapter and use them during your next meeting to increase interactivity. If these work for you, continue to use them. If not, keep experimenting until you find what best fits your unique leadership style.

Chapter 10:
Zoom Your Way to Success

*Strive not to be a success,
but rather to be of value.*
Albert Einstein

While numerous books address the logistical details of leading on Zoom and other video conferencing applications, these platforms are constantly evolving. As a result, how the platform functions today may be very different tomorrow. The best place to start is by taking the provider's training on how to use their platform.

From the Boardroom to the Bedroom

Prior to the COVID-19 pandemic, most webinars and virtual meetings took place in a professional setting. I began leading Continuing Education classes on Zoom for the Texas Association of Realtors (now Texas Realtors) in 2015. The classes met for 12 weeks, one day per week at two different times. We had six locations for our first meeting, and 20 locations for the second meeting.

In order to meet the Texas Real Estate Commission (TREC) requirements for Continuing Education (CE) credit, the instructor was required to be able to see all participants at all times. The instructor setup required two different monitors—one for the slides and one for the camera feed from each location. We were using "speaker view." This meant that when a participant had a question, Zoom would switch from my video feed to the location where the participant was asking a question.

Some Zoom "rooms" had a few people sitting at a conference table. Other rooms could seat up to 50 people. In both instances the setting was professional. The day the next photo was taken we had 10 locations live on Zoom.

When the COVID-19 pandemic hit, workplace environments with ample bandwidth were no longer accessible. Instead, everyone was stuck at home making do with whatever resources they had available. Some participants did their best to look good on camera, but it was just as common to have someone dressed in their pajamas staring blankly back at you from their bedroom. Moreover, if you didn't mute everyone, the background noise was intolerable.

Why Video-Based Virtual Meetings Make Leaders So Uncomfortable

If you are an experienced face-to-face leader or speaker, have you ever wondered why two-way video-conferencing platforms make you so much more uncomfortable than leading in person? Here are three reasons leading any meeting with an interactive video feed can be so disconcerting.

1. **Lack of familiarity with the platform**
   When you led your first face-to-face meeting or class, you probably felt pretty uncomfortable. In fact, many professional speakers still suffer from pre-session jitters even when they have been doing public speaking for years. Part of this discomfort arises from lack of experience with the platform, and of course, the myriad of other potential issues we already discussed.

2. **The camera effect**
   If you have led face-to-face, has your meeting or class ever been recorded? If so, you have already experienced how introducing a camera into the room changed the dynamics completely. Now consider this. If your video-based meeting has 25 participants, you not only have your camera to cope with, but another 25 participant cameras in the room as well.

3. **From one room to many**
   When you lead face-to-face, you and your participants are in a single room. This minimizes the potential for disruption. As mentioned earlier, background noise is a huge issue on all calls and is multiplied by the number of people who are not on mute.

When you use the video conferencing function, you have multiple distractions from multiple rooms. This makes concentrating on your content especially challenging because your brain is wired to notice changes in the environment. This is especially true when a crying child runs into the room, or my personal favorite, the cat jumps in front of the computer and sticks its backside directly in front of the camera.

The Basics

The following overview highlights the most important features to address when leading meetings on video conferencing platforms such as Zoom and Microsoft Teams.

1. **Adjust your audio controls**
   When you first log on, you have the option of muting both your audio feed as well as muting all participants (global mute). It's usually best to have participants join using global mute to limit background noise.

2. **Select a microphone**
   Rather than using your computer's microphone which can create echoes and amplify background noise, we highly recommend using a quality directional microphone that blocks most background noise. As noted earlier, the earbuds for most mobile

devices have effective noise reduction systems that work equally well with your computer.

3. **Select a speaker**
The speakers on your computer are usually adequate for when you are leading, but if you have external speakers, experiment to see what works best for you.

4. **Do a sound check before every meeting**
ALWAYS do a sound check on both your microphone and speakers before launching your meeting. You never know when an external microphone is not plugged in properly, has failed, or, as in my case, the cleaning crew moved my microphone and inadvertently shifted the input channel.

Second, platform providers constantly modify and upgrade their applications. I've personally experienced multiple issues with Zoom in this area. When they do an upgrade, Zoom's default settings often shift. This can also happen when you update your computer's operating system.

Third, doing a sound check is especially important when you are leading on someone else's account. I had a major issue the day before I wrote this chapter where my sound wasn't coming through correctly on my host's Zoom account. Because we did a dry run before the meeting, we were able to troubleshoot the problem which took about 20 minutes.

5. **Select your camera**
If you want to use an external camera, you will have to manually select that option to override the default setting which is normally your device's built-in camera.

6. **Widescreen or "original"?**
If you are presenting on a widescreen video display, it's smart to select the 16:9 Widescreen option if it is available. If not, what Zoom calls the "original" ratio works equally well. Personally, I prefer the original ratio because the smaller size looks better on the Learning Management System (LMS) we use to deliver our online training programs.

7. **Select your video settings**

   If you plan on recording your meetings for replay, record in HD (high definition.) This provides the best quality video. The challenge with HD recordings is they take up tremendous amounts of space on your computer's hard drive or storage system. When I use iMovie to edit, I generally save my recording as "medium" quality (720p). This takes less space and is usually acceptable quality for most online formats.

   Also, different platforms have different options to make your screen look better. Zoom offers an option to touch up your appearance. Microsoft Teams has a cool feature that blurs out your background even when you're joining from an airport, busy office, or your bedroom. Experiment with the various options your platform provider offers and determine which work best for you.

8. **Recording options**

   You have two options for recording your meeting: you can either record to your own computer or to the cloud. I prefer saving my videos on my computer rather than having to go online to access them. If you don't have that much space on your hard drive, however, record to the cloud provided you have sufficient storage capacity in your account.

   As noted in Chapter 9, another decision you must make is whether you want a separate track for the MP4 (video of the meeting) plus a separate track for the audio (MP3 or M4A) for each speaker.

   To illustrate why this is important, when I was shooting the Zoom videos for my Awesome Females in Real Estate Conference, one of my speakers was on a physical inspection in a large apartment building. I was using "speaker view," so all four speakers were visible throughout the recording. Because the broker was having to constantly change locations as the inspection progressed, there was a tremendous amount of visual distraction on her video feed. Fortunately, I had separate audio tracks for each speaker. This made it easier for our video editor to separate the four video feeds and only show the person who was speaking. While the video quality ended up being a bit degraded, the sound quality was excellent.

Real or Virtual Background?

Zoom and Microsoft Teams allow you to create virtual backgrounds from images you upload or from the images they provide. The question is whether you want to use a real or virtual background. If you elect to use a real background, here are some guidelines to follow:

1. **Avoid shooting against a blank wall**
   This can create shadows and wash you out. Look for a background that creates natural depth instead.

2. **Remove background distractions**
   Be sure to declutter and to remove anything that might draw the participants' attention from you to the background. If you have stacks of paper everywhere, put them on the floor or somewhere else where they are out of range from the camera. Also, avoid backgrounds where people in your workplace or family are moving about as you lead your meeting.

3. **Natural light**
   Find a well-lit area, preferably with natural light. It's best to face the window. Avoid sitting next to a window that lights up one side of your face and leaves a shadow on the other side.

   Having a window directly back of you can be tricky. In most cases you will be backlit, which means you will be sitting in a shadow. I've seen a few leaders successfully use a window as a backdrop, but it seldom works well.

4. **Artificial light**
   If you will be relying on artificial light, explore using different types. If you want to look your best, have a professional videographer set up the lighting for you. Alternatively, many leaders have found having one or more LED ring lights to be particularly effective.

Back in 2016 when we were in a rental while building our current home, I used the overhead light with a table lamp on each side of my computer. The three light sources eliminated shadows and cast an even light on my face.

My current office has a large window that throws very strong shadows no matter where I sit. I put a blackout shade over the window. I have multiple light sources in the room: four cans lights, an overhead fixture with incandescent bulbs, and a Lumecube. Overhead lighting usually minimizes wrinkles and other flaws. Natural light shows everything in detail.

5. **Beware of reflective surfaces**
   Mirrors, picture frames, vases, and other glass surfaces can reflect what is happening in the room where you are leading. Eyeglasses often reflect what's on your screen. This creates an instant distraction that can break your connection and lessen engagement. Experiment with adding additional light sources as well as placing your computer at different angles and heights.

While real backgrounds have their drawbacks, so do virtual backgrounds. The biggest issue is that if you don't use a green screen, whenever you move part of your actual background will be visible. It's quite distracting for participants, and depending upon what's in your actual background, can be embarrassing for you as well.

A better option would be to create your own "Zoom Room."

How to Create a "Zoom Room"

Inman News contributor Teresa Boardman made these suggestions about how to set up a "Zoom room."

> *A couple of weeks ago, I decided to up my video meeting presence after seeing myself on camera. I created what I now call my "Zoom room." It takes up a corner in a guest bedroom we no longer use. I took the small writing desk that was facing the wall, turned it around, and moved it a couple of feet from the wall. I hung a piece of green fabric on the wall using green thumbtacks.*

Did you know that you can easily make a green screen from paper, cloth or paint? I made my first one with green tissue paper that I stuffed in holiday gift bags, and I used painter's tape to attach it to the wall.

The green screen makes it possible to use almost any photograph as a background on Zoom. Even though I'm in a small room with my back half a foot away from the wall, I can make it look like I'm anywhere in the world, and wherever I am is well-lit and uncluttered.

I put a couple of books on the desk to raise the level of my laptop or tablet so that I appear as if I'm sitting at a conference room table. Also, that way, my green screen fills the entire frame.

I brought up a work light from the basement and attached it to an old lightweight tripod. I put a paper towel over the light to serve as a softbox and diffuse the light. (Search Google for a clamp-on work light. They cost less than $12.) If you're using a diffuser, choose a light bulb that doesn't give off much heat.

My new setup works well for meeting with anyone, even clients. I look like a pro. Putting it together kept me busy for half-hour or so and gave me a sense of accomplishment, which is always a plus. Using it gives me that feeling of putting a little distance between my professional and personal life.

Thirty Seconds of Challenges

In April 2020, Progressive Insurance did a 30-second commercial beautifully illustrating exactly what can go wrong on video-conferencing meetings. Here's how Progressive described their YouTube video:

"Hey, whoever's doing that, can you go on mute?" The gang is learning how to work from home, and Flo is giving everyone a mouthful.

Here's the blow-by-blow of what went wrong. (You can view the video at: https://www.youtube.com/watch?v=XIhuNFv_P8U)

- The meeting begins with Mara and Jamie talking over each other and debating who should go first.

Zoom Your Way to Success

- Flo can't figure out how to connect or where her camera should be aimed. It's currently aimed at her midsection and she's tugging on her t-shirt.

- There is an echo.

- Flo gets bumped off the meeting and the system shows a black screen that says, "Flo Connecting."

- Jamie goes first and wants to talk about Slide 7, but his audio feed is cutting in and out.

- Rodney jumps in and shouts, "Jamie you're cutting out!"

- Flo reconnects and interrupts Rodney: "I'm sorry I'm late." Her camera is aimed at her nose. Flo then proceeds to adjust her camera with her hand in front of the lens.

- There's a very loud background noise. Lucy interrupts, "Would whoever is doing that go on mute!"

- Allan holds up his mini-vacuum and says, "Oh, my bad."

- Jamie finally gets to the Slide 7, but "DISCOUNT" is misspelled as "DISCOSNOUTS." Jamie pronounces it as "DISCO-SNOUTS" (which now has its own Twitter handle, #DiscoSnouts).

- Rodney jumps back in and says, "I think that's supposed to say, "DISCOUNTS."

- Mara asks Rodney, "Are you sure about that?"

- In the meantime, Flo has been bumped off the meeting again and the black "Flo Connecting" screen is back.

- At the end of the video, Flo is finally back again with her camera aimed at the lower half of her face. She's not certain she's connected and asks, "Hey, can you guys see me?"

Among the comments:

- Thanks for capturing the new office environment! This is how all my Zoom meetings go.

- Real life!

- My last three videoconferences were just like this. They forgot to have someone with an echo put themselves on mute!

- Hilarious, this is exactly what every Zoom meeting looks like everywhere!

- This wasn't funny.

Analyzing What Went Wrong

Before taking a detailed look at what went wrong, how would you have handled these problems if you were leading this meeting? Take a moment to jot down two or three steps you could have used.

Here's our analysis of what went wrong plus some ways to avoid these issues in your meetings.

1. The most important issue is this meeting lacks a leader—someone must be in charge.

2. Sending out "Guidelines for Participants" prior to the meeting would have eliminated many of these issues. This list should include all the guidelines we discussed for audio meetings plus the following items for synchronous video conferencing meetings. (See Appendix A for the complete list.)

    - Check your camera prior to the meeting to make sure it is at eye level.

- Sit in a well-lit location. Avoid sitting in any area that is poorly lit, where there is a bright light source that washes out part of the video feed, or with a window directly in back of you.
- Arrive early and always check your microphone volume before the meeting begins.
- Make sure your name is visible on your video feed as well as the names of all the participants. (This is generally an option either in the general or video settings.)
- Silence your mobile devices. If you have a landline, turn the ringer off. This will avoid interruptions from incoming calls.
- If you have beeps or other sounds to notify you of incoming email, social media notifications, or texts, turn those off on both your computer plus any other mobile devices.
- To minimize bandwidth issues, close all applications on your computer and other devices with the exception of your meeting platform.
- If you decide to use global mute when participants log on but still keep their video feed, advise participants their video will be active, but their audio will be muted when they join. This is especially important for large meetings where background noise is a major issue.
- If you're using global mute, use the "hand-raise" feature to call on those who want to speak. This avoids having people talk over each other.
- If you are not using global mute because you have a small meeting, it's still smart to ask participants to mute themselves in case there is an incoming phone call or other interruption that could disturb other participants. The challenge with this approach, however, is participants often start to speak and fail to realize they are still on mute.

- If you have participants who are unfamiliar with the platform you are using, record a brief video explaining how to use the features you will employ during your meeting. Alternatively, have a second host or moderator available to assist participants in real time.

3. The fact that Flo keeps getting bumped off the meeting may result from her having too many other applications open. As noted earlier, here are some potential fixes:

    - Have the participant close all applications with the exception of their meeting platform.

    - Have them turn off any instant messaging, texts, and their email service as well. Even if they have closed these applications on their computer, they may still appear on their computer if their mobile device and computer are linked together.

    - Many people are unaware that even when they have closed an app, it still may still be running in the background. In my case, I discovered my backup program was refreshing throughout the course of the day and hogging huge portions of my computer's processing capacity. I switched the backup to run late each night and it eliminated the problem.

4. In Jamie's case, you can hear his audio feed cutting in and out. There is also an issue with his video feed as well. Fixes include:

    - Have the participant log off and log back on. This often solves the problem.

    - If that doesn't work, have the participant turn off their video feed. Again, this is where The Six Principles and the other audio-only tips we have covered come into play.

    - Sometimes the bandwidth issue is at the participant's location. This often occurs when there are too many people using their computers and/or mobile devices in the same office/household simultaneously. If this is happening at home, have anyone running more than one device, turn off all their other devices.

- If that doesn't take care of the issue, ask the other people in your location to connect to the internet via their mobile connection (i.e., activate their mobile hotspot) rather than using Wi-Fi.

5. When participants are bored, they often engage in other behaviors such as talking on the phone, having an outside conversation when they believe they're on mute, or in Allan's case, vacuuming in the background. Using global mute eliminates the audio issues.

6. Obviously, no one bothered to review the slides before the meeting. This is why we recommend reviewing your slide deck the evening before as well as the day of the meeting. Otherwise, you can end up with your own version of "Disco-Snouts."

Did you spot anything else?

How to Avoid "Zoom Fatigue"

If at all possible, avoid conducting video conferencing meetings/classes more than three days per week. Being on camera requires tremendous amounts of energy. Many people have started describing the exhausted feeling they're experiencing as "Zoom fatigue" or "Zoom gloom."

Zoom fatigue occurs because humans evolved as social animals who rely on non-verbal, whole body cues to process what is happening around them. When you're staring at a screen, your strongest clue about what is happening with any participant is their face. When you stare at someone too long, however, it can feel threatening or overly intimate.

Furthermore, when your meeting is held in gallery view with multiple screens, your visual processing systems become overloaded with too much input. (Remember, Broca's Area 10 can only process one piece of input at a time.)

Due to information overload during video conferencing meetings, limit these meetings to three days per week if possible. Schedule any other 1:1 meetings by phone or conference call when possible. This means you don't have to be dressed for business and you can take your call from almost anywhere.

If you're someone who dislikes talking on the phone, remember the success of your meeting is tied to the audio portion of the meeting. By spending more time on the phone, you learn to recognize various types of auditory cues such as rate of speech, intonation, and inflection. The result is you will be more effective no matter what type of meeting you lead and will reduce "Zoom gloom" as well.

Four Real Estate Case Studies:
How to Put Zoom to Work in Your Organization

How are large companies and organizations using Zoom and other video conferencing apps in today's environment? The next four case studies from Texas Realtors (formerly The Texas Association of Realtors), *The Wall Street Journal*, EXIT Realty, and Fidelity National Title, illustrate how each of these organizations pivoted during the pandemic to thrive using video-conferencing tools such as Zoom.

Case Study #1 Texas Realtors:
How We Delivered Live CE Training to
500 Locations Simultaneously Using Zoom

Deb Hernandez, Director of Professional Development for Texas Realtors, pioneered the use of Zoom to deliver live Pre-licensing and Continuing Education (CE) classes across Texas in 2012.

At that time, the costs for delivering face-to-face training had become exorbitant, especially given the low number of students enrolling in CE classes. As a way to cut the hemorrhaging, Hernandez searched for a technology solution that would allow the association to deliver live CE remotely and would meet the Texas Real Estate Commission (TREC) requirements for CE.

The biggest hurdle Hernandez faced was persuading TREC to accept a Zoom class as a "live classroom." She made her case by asking,

Can you show me in the rules where it says we cannot use Zoom meetings as a live classroom?

Because TREC was unable to show her where synchronous two-way video did not qualify as a live classroom, Hernandez moved forward using Zoom to deliver "live classroom" CE. This was an extraordinary accomplishment given how stringent CE requirements typically are. TREC requirements include:

- A monitor must track when students check in and check out of the class.

- The monitor must record their real estate license number in order to track their CE credits.

- The student must also provide a picture I.D. such as a driver's license for verification.

- All CE courses require a course outline that must pre-approved by TREC.

- All schools and providers (e.g., real estate brokerages, lenders, title companies, etc.) must also be approved by TREC.

- Names of participants, verification of their identity, their license number, and the course they completed must be submitted to TREC in a timely fashion.

- Providers must keep and maintain accurate records for all classes and participants.

Hernandez launched live "remote" classrooms for both their pre-licensing and CE training. While the enrollments in the pre-licensing classes sputtered, the Continuing Education (CE) enrollments soared. The association later added their Graduate, REALTOR® Institute (GRI) designation to their Zoom offerings.

When the association first began delivering CE, about 40 percent of their attendees used Zoom. As mentioned earlier, I began delivering CE classes for the Texas Realtors in 2015. At that point in time, students had to be physically present at their local association or company in order to receive CE credit and be monitored properly.

When the COVID-19 pandemic began, Hernandez had to pivot from delivering classes at local Realtor associations and companies, to delivering to individual Realtors. The local associations would still handle registrations, checking IDs, monitoring members who were attending classes, and completing the required record keeping.

In April and May of 2020, the association conducted free Code of Ethics class for CE. They had approximately 500 attendees in approximately 500 different locations across Texas. In May 2020, only sixty days after the pandemic began, they had 6,200 enrollments in their Zoom-based classes, far outpacing what they had projected for the year..

As of today, Texas Realtors' Zoom classes have provided a cost-effective way to reach multiple locations across Texas simultaneously for both their CE and GRI courses. The pandemic merely sped up the process they put into play in 2012.

Case Study #2
The Wall Street Journal (WSJ):
Zoom Town Halls and Conventions

New York City was the epicenter of the COVID-19 pandemic in the U.S. Like so many other companies, *WSJ* had to pivot by having their employees work from home. Deborah Falcone, Real Estate Client Partner, explains the challenges they faced.

Like everyone else, we began working from home in the middle of March and holding our regular meetings on Zoom. We soon realized we were losing connection with our advertisers, our audience, and our readers.

We decided to start a town hall series. We seldom get to work closely with our real estate editors, and it turned out to be an incredible opportunity. Mae Cheng, Editor in Chief of our **Mansion Global** *publication, led the effort. During the spring of 2020, we held a number of town halls.*

The first town hall was with a panel of real estate agents. Everyone was so starved for connection, we had 1,000 people from all over the country on our first Zoom meeting. Our panelists described how they were coping with the COVID-19 pandemic as well as the differences they were experiencing in their individual locations.

The town hall was so successful we decided to add four more town halls covering topics our readers wanted such as real estate investment in difficult times, new builders and new developments, etc. Based upon this success, we decided to create a whole series. By fall 2020, the number of attendees had jumped to 3,500 and was continuing to grow.

According to Falcone, the staff at *WSJ* was surprised by how many people wanted to be on the panels. These were people they never anticipated would be eager to participate. Moreover, their subscribers were reaching out to make sure they would be notified when the next town hall would take place.

The response was so positive *WSJ* and *Barron's* decided to conduct their first global real estate conference in fall 2020. Because *WSJ* serves the United States, Europe, and Asia, this was something they had always wanted to do. The challenge prior to the pandemic was the cost for holding the conference as well as the cost to participants to attend. These costs were reduced dramatically with the shift to Zoom.

Our fall 2020 conference included speakers from around the world, members of *WSJ*'s writing staff, their clients, and part of the *News Corp* staff. Falcone believes,

There's no ceiling on what you can do with Zoom and how many people can attend.

Given their successes with Zoom meetings and town halls plus the success of their first ever first international conference, these will likely be a staple at *WSJ* for many years to come.

Case Study #3 EXIT Realty: Leverage Your Zoom Meetings to Provide Better Service and Build Relationships

We have already discussed steps to take before beginning your Zoom meeting. Annette Anthony, Vice President Technology Engagement EXIT Realty, encourages leaders and agents alike to take the following steps to maximize their leverage using Zoom.

Capitalize on the Zoom Registration System

In terms of discovering what matters most to participants prior to your meeting, Anthony recommends using the Zoom registration system. You can collect data about who is attending, ask about what they would like to learn, and accelerate the relationship-building process.

If a real estate agent is conducting a buyer seminar, Anthony suggests collecting the following types of data:

- *Name, email, current property address, phone number, and any other useful data.*

- *Are you a first-time buyer or have you owned a home before?*

- *If you own your current home, when did you purchase it?*

- *Are you in the military where you may qualify for a VA loan or other special loan programs?*

- *Have you met with a lender to check your credit and to see how much you can afford?*

- *If you're thinking about buying, what's your timeline?*

Real estate professionals who gather this data prior to their meetings will find it easier to build the trust and personal connection that motivates participants to do business with them.

You can use this same approach to uncover information about the participants who register for your Zoom meeting. Be sure to obtain their name, contact information, and what they would like to take away from attending your meeting.

Pre-Meeting Steps

Whether you're leading a Zoom meeting inside or outside your organization, Anthony had the following recommendations about maximizing the results from your meeting. For small to medium-sized meetings, especially if they are inside your company or organization:

- Record a quick reminder video and send it out 1-2 days prior to your meeting. Remind participants of the date, time, log-in links as well as how much you are looking forward to meeting with them.

- If this is a mandatory internal meeting, advise participants they will be required to use their video. When participants have an empty box with only their name on it, they often fail to focus on the meeting. As the meeting leader, emphasize you want them to see each other because it strengthens connection within the group. It also forces participants to stay focused on what is happening in the meeting.

- If your meeting is open to people outside your organization, we still recommend encouraging them to join the meeting using their video feed when possible.

- As we have mentioned multiple times, participants joining a meeting using their cellular network often experience bandwidth issues. Turning off the video feed may be their only option for participating.

For large meetings including Zoom webinars:

- Identify a go-to-person, your "communicator," who will provide you with the context you need to deliver the right message for your audience.

- Identify the "cheerleader." This is the person who will rally participants to register for the event and will also play an integral part in your post-meeting follow up.

- If you're leading a webinar on Zoom, you can insert your brand in the registration and login links. You can also add photos, information about your meeting, and much more. Visit the Zoom Help Center for detailed instructions on how to customize your offerings.

- Use the Zoom dashboard to export your list of attendees. Enter this data into your CRM (Client Relationship Management) system or into an Excel spreadsheet where you can track attendance. This allows you to systematically follow-up after your meeting.

- Send out a brief teaser video with at least one benefit participants will obtain from attending meeting or class. It's an excellent way to provide participants with another reason to attend.

- Be sure to share the registration link in your teaser video. To make sure they receive your information, email, text, and/or use the social media messengering apps. This matters because participants don't always open their emails, especially if it ends up in their spam filter.

As the meeting ends

Here are Anthony's recommendations about what to do as the meeting ends:

- As the meeting ends, ask participants to use the "hand raise" feature to answer the question, "How many of you took notes today?" Anthony says lots of hands normally go up.

- Next, have participants look over their notes and circle one thing they would be willing to implement in their business after the meeting.

- Encourage participants to leverage what they learned as a way to provide better customer service or by posting it on social media if it would assist clients with their business or organization.

After the meeting
Anthony explains how she shares her Zoom recording with three different audiences. Here's what she recommends:

- For those who attend the meeting I send them a video message saying,

    Thank you for attending. I really appreciate you being with us. I'd love to hear your takeaways. By the way, here's the recording.

    Provide the link where they can view or download the video.

- For the second audience that registered and did not attend, create a second video message that says:

    We had a great event and noticed you didn't make it. Sometimes people have a sick child at home, they don't feel well themselves, or have another commitment. We recorded the session and I would like to send it to you. Please call me back and let me know where to send the recording.

Anthony has experienced tremendous success using the following approach:

Imagine the impact you create when you notice someone did not attend and you then offer to send them the recording of the meeting. Most people call back, especially

> when you inquire if something was wrong that caused them to miss the meeting.

- The third audience are people you know personally and who would benefit from your content but did not register for the meeting. You can share your video via email or on their social media accounts.

Anthony's final take away is this:

> Remember, there's no piece of technology that will ever replace you has a human. When you're excited to see your participants, they're more excited to see you.

Case Study #4
Fidelity National Title Agency:
Connect and Have Fun

Dena Jones, director of Strategic Partnerships and assistant vice president for Fidelity National Title Agency in Phoenix, Arizona, explains why Zoom is such a powerful lead generation and lead conversion platform:

> A major benefit our clients have reported about using Zoom is how quickly they have been able to build rapport by creating highly focused, intentional quality conversations. This has allowed them to establish trust at a much higher level and ultimately generate even more new and referral business.

When the pandemic struck, Fidelity had to transition 18,000 employees in 1,600 different locations from working face-to-face to working at home in only two weeks. As Jones observed, "I had to get really good at Zoom really fast."

Like most other organizations, Fidelity began using Zoom for daily internal team meetings. A major part of their business, however, comes from providing education to the real estate community. Jones says Fidelity quickly pivoted and began offering their real estate education online using Zoom.

Make Your Backgrounds Ultra-Personal

As Jones focused on maintaining connection with her company's clients, she searched for fun and creative ways to do so.

One of the things I love about the backgrounds is how you can make your meetings ultra-personal. By customizing the background, you can connect people with people in a surprising way that makes them feel like they're with you physically.

Here are several examples of how Jones did this:

Title companies have always hosted lunch and learns and held happy hours as a way to serve the Realtor community. While we hosted several virtual happy hours, we decided to hold a virtual "Yappy Hour." We invited our clients to bring their pets to our Zoom meeting, grab their beverage of choice, and introduce their pet to the group. It was great seeing everyone since so many people wanted to connect, but most of all, it was really fun meeting everyone's pet.

In the previous slide, you can see how Jones customized her background for her Virtual Yappy Hour event.

One of my themes last spring was quarantine costuming where I wore a different costume every day. It definitely created some interesting reactions and it made people smile as we began our meetings. Going virtual required us to engage in a different way and having fun made it easier.

Fidelity National Title Agency serves not only real estate brokers and agents, they also have a robust business serving developers. Jones has been conducting "New Home Virtual Showcases" where Fidelity features three different new home subdivision tours via Zoom. They also post the showcases on Facebook Live each month. The goal is to showcase what the lifestyle would be like for people who decide to purchase in these locations. The next two examples illustrate how Jones created an ultra-personalized Zoom background.

As we toured through the construction at the new Ritz Carlton coming to Paradise Valley, I was able to use Zoom to put myself right in the lobby virtually, even though the property was still under construction.

When Jones selects what to highlight in her Zoom backgrounds, she recommends searching for features that make the property unique, such as the "super garage" in the following slide that can accommodate an SUV with a boat and a large RV as well. Also notice how she dropped in a quotation in the upper left-hand corner of her screen.

Zoom Your Way to Success

As Jones explains:

Our Zoom video tours have been getting great traction with real estate agents and their clients. When people are unable to see these communities in person, this is an excellent way for them to experience what the lifestyle will be like, what it will feel like when the community center is built, and to experience the other amenities.

Our clients have also started using Zoom with their buyers and sellers. I have one client who is planning a virtual bingo event on Zoom and another who is leading virtual yoga classes. Zoom is a safe platform to bring people together, especially when everybody is so starved for connection.

Jones' creative approach to having fun on Zoom is a great way to banish Zoom gloom!

Chapter 10 Key Points

1. Regardless of the whether the meeting platform you are using accommodates video, the audio is still primary due to the large percentage of participants who join meetings from mobile devices or who have bandwidth issues.

2. The shift from "the boardroom to the bedroom," has made virtual meetings harder to lead due to the "camera effect" and having to manage multiple room environments rather than a single room.

3. Always check the audio before every meeting. You never know when there may be an issue with your microphone or the system settings.

4. Experiment with different types of backgrounds, or better yet, set up a "Zoom room."

5. Send out a "Guidelines for Participants" prior to your meeting (or prior to the first session of a class or a meeting that repeats regularly).

6. Minimize bandwidth issues by closing all other applications on your computer and turning off all notifications. If necessary, you may need to ask others who are sharing the same internet connection to only have a single device open at a time or to use their phone as a hot spot rather than your Wi-Fi.

7. When participants have bandwidth issues, advise them to turn off their camera and to participate using "audio-only."

8. Avoid "Zoom fatigue/Zoom gloom" by limiting the number of video conferencing meetings you hold to three days a week if possible.

9. The four case studies provide real world examples of how large organizations are using Zoom as a way to conduct their business, provide virtual education, maintain personal connection, and better serve their clients and users.

10. Identify which strategies from this chapter are appropriate for how you lead your meetings and experiment with implementing at least one of them on your next virtual meeting.

Chapter 11:
Leading in the Dark

*The task of the leader is to get their
people from where they are to
where they have not been.*
Henry Kissinger

Dealing with multiple cameras, multiple rooms, and multiple distractions on video-conferencing platforms creates one set of problems. Leading webinars, recording your virtual meetings for replay, and delivering on avatar-based platforms creates an entirely different sets of issues. When you are leading alone without the benefit of a moderator or co-host and no opportunity to interact live with your participants, it's just you, your slide deck, and the little green camera light. When there is no interaction with your participants, it's the equivalent of "leading in the dark."

The Monologue Challenge: Building Engagement During Asynchronous Meetings

When you're "leading in the dark" your session can easily become a monologue. Depending upon whether your meeting is live (synchronous) or you are recording it for replay (asynchronous), add as many engagement elements as possible. This is especially important for asynchronous meetings where there is no live interactivity. Here are seven ways to ramp up participant engagement using the audio feed.

1. **Have a co-presenter**
   Lengthy monologues are the kiss of death for any virtual meeting. Using a co-presenter is an excellent solution. To illustrate this point, television, podcasts, and radio talk show monologues run for several minutes followed with two-way conversations with guests or callers. Remember, the human brain is wired to focus on changes in the environment. When there is no interactivity with participants, two voices are better than one.

2. **Pace**

   As we discussed in Chapter 8, a pace of approximately 160 words per minute is about right for most virtual meetings. In terms of your slide deck, your pace will vary based upon the type of session you are leading. In live meetings you can leave a single slide up for a long period of time because your audience is focused on you. In contrast, webinars work best at about one slide per minute. The faster pace on asynchronous sessions helps to maintain participant attention.

   If your session will be delivered on a Learning Management System (LMS), a pace of 2-3 slides per minute is about right. While this can be distracting when you're doing a live session, leaving a single slide up for a full minute during an asynchronous meeting can seem like an eternity for your participants.

3. **Music**

   In a session based upon my book *The PQ Factor: Stop Resisting and Start Persisting*, I discuss how to synch your brain with your favorite music. I use the following slide to introduce the concept.

   I then play three different clips of music with three different beats. (Note the audio icon on the slide.) When I conduct this session face-to-face, I ask the group which beat they liked best. On live webinars and video conferencing meetings, you can use the hand raise or polling features to determine participant preferences. If your session is not live and you have data from past sessions, share the data on previous participant response rates.

To wrap up this segment, the takeaway is:

If you're having a bad day or feeling out of synch, put your brain in top performance mode by listening to a few minutes of your favorite music. Your favorite beat synchronizes both sides of your brain with each other and you'll definitely feel better.

Whenever possible, choose examples that enhance your participants' understanding of the topic or provide some other benefit.

4. **Sound effects**

Another excellent way to break up your monologue is to use sound effects. For example, one of my friends likes to wrap up her sessions by telling her audience to go out and ROAR! You could combine an image like the following one with an audio clip of a lion roaring.

There are a number of online sites that provide sound effects. For example, Storyblocks https://www.storyblocks.com has over

60 different categories of sound effects including animals, boats, city, clocks, crowds, nature, office, people, phones, sports, traffic, water, and weather.

As you prepare the content for your asynchronous meeting, review some of the sound effects to see how they may fit with your topic. For example, if you were doing a session on time management, you could pair the following image with the sound of a ticking clock or an alarm going off.

Always build audio or video clips directly into your individual slides. Never count on the internet to play anything live. To add a sound clip to your slide, all you have to do is to import the MP3 file into the appropriate slide and play by clicking the audio icon (adjacent to the clock in the previous slide).

Depending upon the delivery platform you are using, you may have to adjust the settings to hear the audio embedded in your slide. To test this, go to a slide with an embedded audio or video clip. Click on the audio play button on the slide. Listen to the entire clip to make sure the sound is clear. If you are working with a video editor, we recommend inserting the original audio or video track directly into the recording rather than loading it into your slide deck because both the visual and the sound quality will be better.

Leading in the Dark

5. **Share what's odd, unusual, or unexpected**

 The next two slides are based upon Daniel Amen's book, *Making a Good Brain Great.* According to Amen, many people struggle to keep negative thoughts from repeating over and over in their minds. He calls these "ANTS—Automatic Negative Thoughts." The next slides introduce the concept of an "ANT" invasion and what you can do about it.

I end this segment by explaining Amen's research has shown the best way to create your personal "ANT-eater" and eliminate "ANTS" is to write them down.

6. **Tell a story**

Most top speakers are excellent story-tellers. Stories provide a change of pace from the content in your slides. If you want to become better at story-telling, start with something funny that happened to you. For example:

Have you ever been so focused on one task that you misplaced your keys or some other item? Last night I was talking on the phone with a friend who was really upset. I didn't realize until later that while we were talking, I put the milk away in the microwave.

While some people may attribute this to getting older, young people make these types of mistakes as well. The reason this happens is due to an area called Broca's Area 10, which the neuroscientists have nicknamed "Mother." "Mother," which is part of the Reticular Activating System, can only focus on one thought at a time.

When I put the milk in the microwave, my left brain was consciously focused on what my friend was saying. My right brain knew the milk needed to be put away, but its vocabulary only consists of a few words such as your name. It has no understanding milk should be stored where it would be "cold."

This simple story works for the following reasons.

- It opens with a "you" question inquiring about something almost everyone has experienced—misplacing their keys.

- Two common explanations are provided. While putting the milk in the microwave could be linked to cognitive decline, it's much more likely to be due to "Mother" being focused on the issue the friend was having.

- While the leader/instructor could simply define what "Mother" does, the story provides a memory hook by tying the story to the listener's personal experience. This increases the probability the listener will recall what "Mother" does.

- The leader can then segue into reasons why driving while texting is so dangerous because "Mother" can only process incoming information one piece at a time. Putting it bluntly, it's the equivalent of driving with a blood alcohol level of 1.2. (Drunk driving is considered to be a blood alcohol level of .08 and above.) If your conscious brain is focused on texting, it's not paying attention to your driving.

Peppering one or two short personal stories into your session provides important variability in your audio track. If you want to become more effective at using stories in your meetings, consider joining Toastmasters or the National Speakers' Association (NSA) where you can hone both your story-telling and speaking skills.

7. **Videos**

Videos are an excellent way to bring variety to your asynchronous sessions, eliminate the monologue challenge, while also adding visual variety. Any funny, unusual, or highly engaging video can quickly recapture a participant's errant attention. In general, 15-60 second video clips are the most effective.

To avoid having copyright problems, shoot your own videos or use video licensing sites such as AdobeStock, Dreamstime, iStock, ShutterStock, Storyblocks, etc. Look for sites that allow you to license a specific number of downloads rather than paying for each video individually.

In terms of using YouTube videos, do so at your own risk. You need a release from the creator, especially if your session will be available to the public or is for commercial use. If the creator used any licensed images, you will also need a separate license to use those images. Otherwise, you could end up like we did—paying $650.00 to Getty Images for copyright infringement when a freelancer we hired used one of their licensed images and didn't advise us.

Vary Your Visuals to Keep Participants Engaged

In addition to the seven strategies for adding variety to your audio track, here are 11 additional suggestions for increasing engagement when "leading in the dark" by using video and providing additional types of variety to your slides.

1. **Use "gallery view"**
   Greg McDaniel and Matt Johnson, the co-hosts of the Real Estate Uncensored podcast, decided to track their engagement statistics when they used "gallery view" (where you see both hosts and their guest) vs. "speaker view" (where only the speaker who is talking is visible). Their viewers overwhelmingly preferred gallery view.

   When you're listening to a conversation in person, your brain naturally views the entire room, not a single speaker at a time—this is what gallery view creates. Furthermore, "speaker view" often shifts the video feed to the wrong person—sometimes it's even one of the participants!

2. **Use the animation feature**
   As noted in Chapter 7, for slides with more than one bullet point, use the animation feature to bring up one bullet point at a time, rather than displaying all the bullet points simultaneously. The same approach applies to pictures and graphs.

   You can also use different types of animations to make your slides appear differently. For example, Microsoft PowerPoint offers over 30 different slide entry styles as part of their animation feature. Avoid using more than one or two different entry styles in a single presentation because it can become a distraction.

3. **Photos**
   There are an infinite number of ways to use photos to engage your participants visually and to support what you're saying on the audio. Here are some additional examples:

The previous slide introduces how real estate agents can convert more listing appointments into signed listings. I follow it up with a discussion of the "Premium Marketing Plan" in the following illustration. The businesspeople racing slide provides a quick segue into the detailed discussion about how to use the Premium Marketing Plan.

Premium Marketing Plan for the Property Located at: _____

Courtesy of _____

16 Key Strategies to Net You the Most Money from Your Sale	My Co	1	2	3
1. The Four "P's" all agents do: put up a yard sign, post your listing online, on MLS, and market it in print.	√			
2. Charity: we donate 10 percent of net profits on every deal	√			
3. Chatbot rapid response lead converter captures leads and schedules showings 24-7.	√			
4. Comprehensive disclosure system and written seller service guarantee minimize your exposure to costly litigation.	√			
5. Customized print marketing includes targeted, niche strategies with Just Listed and Just Sold cards.	√			
6. Lifestyle marketing strategy highlights benefits of living in your area.				
7. Matterport 3D and Virtual Reality property tour	√			
8. National buyer and seller relocation network	√			
9. Open House (traditional & broker) with refreshments and Spacio instant conversion system.	√			
10. Predictive Analytics CMA adjusts for upgrades and appraisals for the most accurate pricing possible.	√			
11. Single property website and Facebook business page using the seller's address as the URL.	√			
12. Social media marketing plan posts your listing on Facebook business page, Marketplace, Instagram, Pinterest, YouTube, and other social media sites.	√			
13. Smart Homeowner system: manuals, repairs, parts, and recall notices for all your appliances.	√			
14. Staging services to make your home look its best.	√			
15. True cost of homeownership tool.	√			
16. Listing posted in 18 languages online & on Facebook.	√			

- The next slide illustrates two approaches to ending struggle and procrastination. The first strategy is the "one-pushup-a-day" approach where you commit to doing only one pushup daily. Of course, when you do one pushup, you're likely to do more.

    The second approach is to take "baby steps," which produce in big results over time.

- You can also couple a surprising observation with a photo illustrating your point. The following slide is from a session on differences in male and female communication styles. The slide is based upon the book, *Men Are Like Waffles and Women Are Like Spaghetti* by Bill and Pam Farrell.

Leading in the Dark

Most men process information in small, separate chunks (hence the waffle). Women often string together multiple thoughts (spaghetti) that men often have trouble following.

There are two takeaways. First, if you want to communicate more effectively with both men and women via email, use concise bullet points, avoid using emojis, and long rambling sentences. Second, if you're scheduling an appointment, give the recipient a choice between two specific time slots. If those times don't work, most people will get back to you with an alternative time.

- The following two slides are from a social media marketing session. Instead of listing all the great things about the local lifestyle as a series of bullet points, the visuals are much more compelling.

4. **Blank backgrounds and screens**

A number of photo licensing sites have photos with a blank screen embedded within them. This allows you drag and drop a photo on the blank screen or to embed your own text. In the next slide discussing how to use Facebook private groups, I did a screen capture of our Awesome Females in Real Estate group page and dropped it into the blank iPad screen.

There are also applications that will let you drop photos into a photo. I dropped the cover image of *The PQ Factor* into the following slide.

Leading in the Dark

The next slide illustrates six different types of screens from Clipart.com. You can drop in your own text, quotations, pictures, or graphics depending what type of screen you use. If you use a background with a lot of detail, limit the amount of text you use. Also, if the screen is displayed at an angle, you can rotate your text box to fit the angle of the screen.

The next slide is from a session on how to create an effective marketing campaign. The old-fashioned strategy of getting your name out there using bus stops, billboards, shopping carts, etc. doesn't work well in today's environment.

The image of the bus stop had a blank screen. I added the photo of the woman talking on the phone to represent the Realtor and a text box to provide her name and phone number. The process is simple. Drag and drop the original image into your slide, and you can then drop additional images on top of the first image and/or use a text box.

5. Use separate images for individual concepts

The next three slides address three of our "Ten Internet Rules of the Road." Rather than listing the rules in bullet points, use a separate visual for each concept. This makes the concepts easier to remember and is especially important when you are preparing your session for delivery on an LMS.

Leading in the Dark

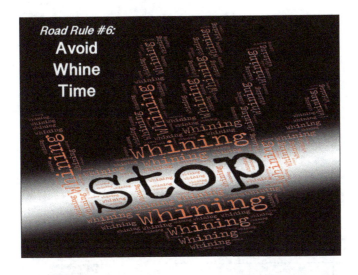

6. **Bring a smile to their face**

There are numerous ways to make your participants smile. Slides with cute kids, funny animals, or an unexpected twist are particularly effective. You can also use an off-the-wall photo or video, especially if it relates in some way to the point you're making.

Here are some examples:

7. Treat a familiar topic in an unexpected manner

I often reference books in my training. While you could use a screenshot of the book's cover, these can be blurry on large screens plus the cover artwork is copyrighted. Fortunately, it's easy to create your own take on the title.

For example, in my business planning class I recommend Brian Tracy's book, *Eat that Frog*. In terms of your daily to-do list, I urge participants to complete the biggest, ugliest task of the day first. Here's the slide I normally use.

If you really wanted to drive home the "yuck" factor associated with some tasks, the next slide certainly would do it.

8. **Quizzes**

We discussed quizzes in Chapter 7. The following quiz opens a segment on how participants can increase the number of people who view their social media posts by being "you-focused," rather than "me-focused."

What percentage of your posts should be about you and your business?

a. 5 percent
b. 25 percent
c. 50 percent
d. 75 percent
e. 90 percent

What percentage of your posts should be about you and your business?

a. **5 percent**
b. 25 percent
c. 50 percent
d. 75 percent
e. 90 percent

9. **Graphics**

Using graphics is another way to vary your content and increase engagement. The next two slides use graphics from Dreamstime.com.

Sometimes you will be unable to find a graphic to match your content. If you're using PowerPoint, remember to check "Design Ideas" for suggested layouts.

For example, I needed a slide to illustrate how commonalities lead to connections, how connections lead to trust, and how when people trust you, they are more likely to do business with you.

If you are using a custom template for your slides, Design Ideas will only generate variations based upon your template. To generate the maximum amount of responses, open a new file without a template and enter only the words you want to use to describe the concept.

Here are two examples Design Ideas generated, the second one being a 15-second video where the clouds were moving across the sky in back of the buildings.

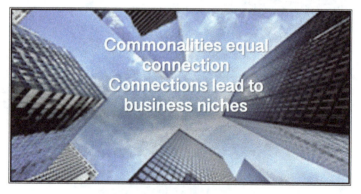

10. Create graphs using Microsoft Excel or Apple Numbers spreadsheets

Both Microsoft's Excel and Apple's Numbers allow you to create various types of graphs from within their spreadsheet programs This includes bar graphs, line graphs, pie charts, etc.

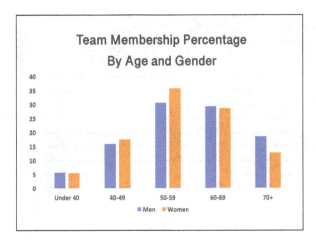

11. Quotations

Rather than displaying a quote with a plain background, find an image that supports your point. When you find a quotation you like, search online for images using the quotation. Rather than copying someone else's slide, however, create your unique take on the quotation. The following slide was taken from a session on the importance of self-care. Note the variation in the fonts for emphasis.

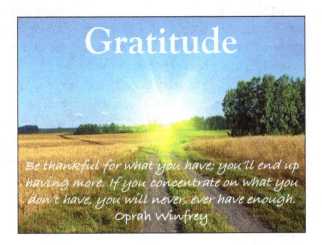

I used the next slide to wrap up a recent keynote I delivered via Zoom. The graphic clearly illuminates the path forward for participants while simultaneously highlighting the Zig Ziglar quotation.

As we have said repeatedly throughout this book, every session you lead is a chance for you to grow your leadership skills.

Learning Management Systems (LMS)

What is an LMS? According to Wikipedia:

A learning management system (LMS) is a application for the administration, documentation, tracking, reporting, automation and delivery of educational courses, training programs, or learning and development programs. The learning management system concept emerged directly from e-learning. Although the first LMS appeared in the higher education sector, the majority of the LMSs today focus on the corporate market.

The purpose of an LMS is to deliver and manage all types of content, including video, courses, and documents. In the education and higher education markets, an LMS will include a variety of functionality that is similar to corporate but will have features such as rubrics, teacher and instructor facilitated learning, a discussion board, and often the use of a syllabus. A syllabus is rarely a feature in the corporate LMS, although courses may start with heading-level index to give learners an overview of topics covered.

Which LMS is right for you or your organization?
If you're leading courses for a school, corporation, or other large entity, you will probably be required to use their LMS platform. If you have

to select your own LMS, there are numerous online reviews comparing various systems. If you're only going to create courses by recording a video and then loading it into the LMS, most systems are adequate for that purpose.

If you are searching for an enterprise system, make sure you do an apples-to-apples comparison in terms of costs. Many LMSs have additional fees on top of what they advertise as their base price. Determine which bells and whistles you need as well as the best value for your budget.

Key points you need to know as you design LMS courses
LMSs share a great deal in common with webinars. In fact, the most robust LMSs allow you to lead live classes using GoToWebinar, GoToTraining, and WebEx. Nevertheless, here are some key differences to note as you design courses to deliver on any LMS platform.

- Break your session into bite-sized chunks of 3-7 minutes per section.

- Use more slides. Instead of a pace of one slide per minute which is a common pace for webinars and live sessions, 2-3 slides per minute works best for an LMS. While this creates more work for you as the course creator, it definitely increases engagement. For slides with bullet points, using the slide entry feature for each point enhances engagement and has the same impact as a separate slide.

- Use as many of the tools from this chapter as practical to keep your session moving and users engaged.

Case Study

I began searching for a Learning Management System for our training business back in 2011. After looking at numerous companies, a friend introduced me to the DigitalChalk (DC) LMS in 2014. It was everything I had searched for and much more. Here are the key features that have kept us with DC, even as the number of LMS providers exploded:

- Available 24-7 on demand, with users being able to immediately access the training as soon as they register and pay the registration fee.

- No requirement to download additional software.

- Reasonably priced.

- Complete e-commerce system including full credit card processing system at minimal cost. This frees us up from managing credit cards and collecting money from our users. The system immediately notifies us when someone enrolls. At the end of the month, DC sends us a monthly report with our new users along with a direct deposit of our proceeds to our bank account.

- Robust systems for tracking individual student progress and other administrative functions.

- Authoring tools enabling us to maximize interactivity for asynchronous classes.

- "Chapters" feature when programmed correctly, allows users to quickly locate any part of the session they would like to review.

- Excellent customer and tech support by phone, not chat.

- The ability to create links to track affiliate referrals and create discount coupons.

- Single sign-on capability allowing our clients to white label our courses and deliver them on their intranet.

- SCORM compliant (i.e., meets the reporting requirements to deliver Continuing Education courses).

Whether you're conducting a live training, a webinar, or creating a training video, in most cases your participants are "one and done." Trying to locate the two-minute segment you really wanted to hear again requires clicking and playing back different locations in the video. Very few users are willing to put up with the hassle. It's not only annoying, it can be a time waster as well.

The most important feature to our clients, however, is documenting user activity. This is one of the reasons for using a robust LMS for asynchronous delivery, because users can repeat specific aspects of each module as many times as they would like.

The following screen capture displays how DC's Gradebook Feature tracks each user's progress. The far-right hand column shows how many times this user opened each module. Note this user opened Session #15, The Pre-Listing Package seven times!

This type of spaced, repetitious learning produces significant results. Our clients consistently report their new agents who complete this course succeed, while those who fail to complete it almost always exit the business.

Session	Status	Date	Count
Session 4: How to Create and Grow a Referral ...	Passed	06/16/20	(2)
Session 5: Open Up to Open House Part 1	Passed	06/17/20	(1)
Session 5: Open Up to Open House Part 2	Passed	06/17/20	(2)
Session 6: Create a Print Marketing Campaign ...	Passed	06/18/20	(2)
Session 7: Digital Marketing Strategies for N...	Passed	07/01/20	(3)
Session 8: Lights, Camera, Action!	Passed	07/09/20	(3)
Session 9: Social Media Lead Conversion--The ...	Passed	07/21/20	(2)
Session 10: Working with Buyers	Passed	07/21/20	(1)
Session 11: The Buyer Interview in Depth	Passed	07/21/20	(3)
Session 12: Negotiation Basics	Passed	07/21/20	(1)
Session 13: Set the Stage for a Successful Sh...	Passed	07/21/20	(1)
Session 14: Writing an Offer You Can Take to ...	Passed	07/30/20	(3)
Session 15: The Pre-Listing Package	Passed	09/02/20	(7)
Session 16: Listing Appointment Day: The Eigh...	Passed	09/16/20	(1)
Session 17: Overcoming Seller Listing Objecti...	Passed	09/17/20	(2)
Session 18: Offer Negotiation Strategies	Passed	09/17/20	(1)
Session 19: Negotiating Multiple Offers	Passed	09/22/20	(2)
Session 20: Advanced Lead Generation: Expired...	Passed	09/24/20	(6)
Session 21: Managing and Closing the Transact...	In progress	10/02/20	(2)

Two custom DC features that increase user interaction

The following screen displays the DC Course Creation tool. There are two key features in this platform that allow course creators to dramatically increase user interaction with the program.

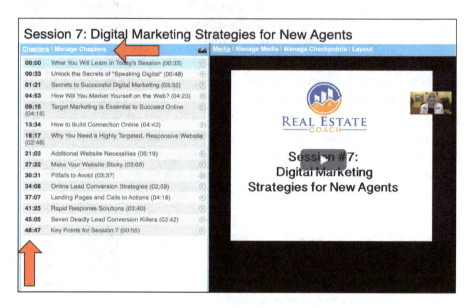

The first feature is the "Manage Chapters" feature. I use this feature to program the beginning and end points of each segment in the session. While this requires additional work, it makes it extremely easy for the user to locate the exact part of the session they want to listen to again. This is the primary reason so many of our users revisit different parts of the program repeatedly. Note the bulk of the segments are about 3-4 minutes in length.

Building interactivity into your courses

The most powerful tool for building interactivity into our DC classes are the "checkpoints." The following slide illustrates how checkpoints display when used with a quiz.

Leading in the Dark

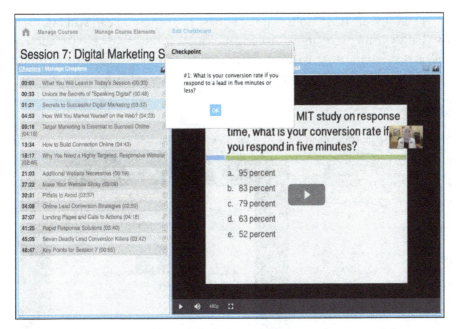

Since there is no polling or hand-raise feature when you deliver your course asynchronously, the checkpoints stop the program from playing and require the user to interact before proceeding with the program. Checkpoints work especially well in conjunction with the chapter titles as a way to segment the module and reinforce learning as well. The next screen capture illustrates how the six "checkpoints" are programmed.

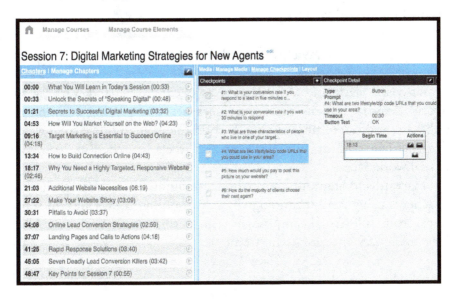

Lead Great Virtual Meetings

Even if your LMS does not have these features, you can still ask users to "Pause your player now" to engage in an interactive activity such as the action steps they will take from your session or how they might apply a specific learning point you have just covered.

While there is definitely a learning curve in terms of using any LMS, courses created on these platforms can have a shelf-life that lasts for several years. For you as the course creator, it is "one and done" until you decide to update the course.

Avatar-Based-Platforms

Avatar-based-platforms (ABPs) such as Second Life and Virbela are hybrid delivery systems that combine aspects of gaming technology, webinars, and video conferencing. Second Life is an online virtual world that first launched in June 2003, while Virbela launched in 2012 as a virtual workplace.

Harvard and Stanford Universities are among the increasing number of schools using ABP technology to deliver online classes and, in some cases, create full virtual campuses as well. Businesses are also using ABPs for conferences, meetings, and training.

Julian Depauw, Head of Academic Innovation for the EGADE Business School in Monterey Mexico, described how they are using Virbela to deliver a quarter of their MBA classes:

> *We needed an improved virtual experience, where instead of being passive listeners, students transformed into active players and game-changers. With Virbela our students now create their avatars, explore our virtual campus, and dance Zumba, all while receiving a cutting-edge education. This gamification approach to education has boosted the virtual EGADE experience in all aspects.*

Currently, eXp Realty has over 40,000 agents and they conduct almost all of their business virtually on Virbela, with the exception of face-to-face meetings with their clients.

Conducting meetings and classes on ABPs

As with any other virtual meeting platform, the audio is still primary. Depending upon which features you activate, you can run your ABP session as an interactive teleclass, like a webinar where you're engaging participants with the hand raise feature, or like a Zoom meeting where the speaker's slides and/or videos are displayed on an embedded screen in the "meeting room."

The following screen illustrates what a Virbela classroom looks like including how slides and videos are displayed. The blue circles indicate where participants can have private conversations. You can interact with the instructor in one of the three ways: unmuting your microphone and interacting live, by raising your hand to ask a question or make a comment, or by using the chat.

The next slide illustrates the Virbela breakout meeting rooms. Although the following screen capture doesn't display it, the same interactive features as the classrooms are available in the meeting rooms as well.

The next slide shows how slide decks and videos appear when they're embedded as part of a presentation. This screen capture is from the auditorium.

Challenges leading on ABPs

Needless to say, there are a variety of unique challenges associated with delivering in the ABP environment. Here are some of the most common ones:

1. There is a learning curve for your participants that includes how to navigate within the platform and customizing their avatar. To illustrate this point, several weeks before I wrote this chapter, I was selected to moderate my first panel on the Virbela ABP. I asked my panelists to join me on Virbela to make sure they were familiar with how to enter and exit from the stage. I also planned on doing our panel prep during that meeting as well.

    Unfortunately, my panelists had issues logging on as well as working with their avatars. After about 25 minutes of hassles, I decided to move our panel prep over to a conference call.

    The first day of the conference, it became painfully clear the ABP-experience was comparable to leading an audio-only teleclass or conference call with the added distraction of having a screen full of avatars, a number of which were ending up on the stage and other places they didn't belong.

2. Presenters were unable to advance their own slides during the main sessions. While Virbela had two concierge assistants in the room who jumped in to advance the slides, hearing the speaker repeatedly saying, "Next slide," was less than optimal. The breakout sessions had the same problem as well.

3. The sound quality of the live speakers was acceptable, however, the sound quality for videos embedded within presentations was much poorer quality.

4. The most disappointing part of the conference occurred during one of the breakout sessions. One of the keynote speakers was unable to load her slides into the platform and was totally unprepared to present without them. After waiting 35 minutes hoping she would at least give us some key points as we waited, I left the session.

As we have advised you throughout this book, be prepared to lead your meeting or class in an audio-only format. You can always share your slides, handout, or notes afterwards.

5. The funniest part of the conference was the "disembodied heads." The red arrow in the next slide points to one of the participant's avatars that managed to appear on stage as a disembodied head during a main session.

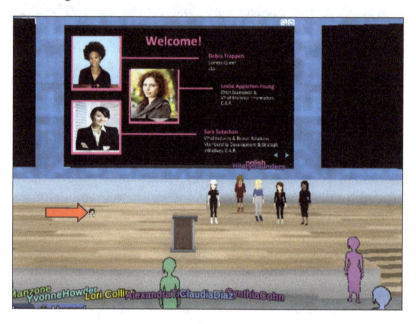

The "disembodied heads" also showed up during the breakout sessions. When some participants were unable to figure out how to have their avatars face the presentation screen, they clicked on "room configuration tab." The result was either all the chairs in the room disappeared and everyone was left standing or those who were sitting ended up with their heads sticking out of the floor. Fortunately, the moderators quickly corrected the issue. Even so, everyone still had to find a place to sit a second time.

Key steps to take when leading on an ABP

If you will be using an ABP, make sure you complete these steps prior to meeting day.

1. More than any other platform, delivering live sessions on an ABP requires detailed preparation. Make sure you are completely familiar with the features of the ABP you will be using to lead your session.

2. Advise your participants it can take 30 minutes or longer for them to download the ABP software, set up their avatar, and to figure out how to navigate on the site. Send that reminder at least two or three times.

3. If you are embedding videos or sound effects into your slide deck, check the sound quality prior to your session. Any time you embed video from a different source into an ABP, the video and audio quality will be poorer quality than the original. This is true on Zoom and on LMSs as well.

4. Be prepared for errant avatars wandering around in your meeting room, disembodied heads, cross-talk on the ABP platform, and a slew of other potential issues. Stay focused on your participants and correct whatever issues you can as quickly as possible.

5. Give participants your agenda, handout, or the link where they can download the slides from your session. If you don't send these out prior to the meeting, make sure you post them in the chat with a link where participants can download them.

6. For every virtual meeting you lead, always be prepared to lead with no visuals. In other words, think "teleclass." As mentioned earlier when my internet went down due to a thunderstorm, I was able to rejoin the meeting and wrap up the webinar by phone. What made this possible was providing the handout prior to the meeting.

    If you don't have a handout, you can ask questions and have an interactive discussion with your participants by unmuting their microphones or using the chat to field questions. Take notes and share them with your participants after the meeting.

7. ALWAYS have a backup plan. When things go wrong, avoid becoming frustrated. Accept this is part of leading classes and meetings virtually. When you can view the challenges you face as learning opportunities, it becomes much easier to cope.

The bottom line is no matter what type of platform you use for your virtual meeting, there will be challenges. Be as prepared as possible, have a backup plan, and when you do encounter an issue, smile and cope with it as best you can.

Chapter 11 Key Points

1. If you're leading an asynchronous virtual meeting with no opportunity for live interaction, you can still drive participant engagement by using any of the 18 strategies outlined in this chapter for varying your auditory and video feed.

2. In order to avoid monologues add music, sound effects, video, or have a co-presenter.

3. Increase participant engagement by using pictures, graphics, and humor.

4. Learning Management Systems are the best delivery platforms available for conducting 24-7 on-demand, self-paced asynchronous virtual meetings that support distributed learning and participant engagement.

5. Avatar-Based-Platforms are currently the most challenging leadership platform to master due to the distractions from errant avatars plus the learning curve for both leaders and participants. Detailed preparation is mandatory.

Chapter 12:
Which Principles and Tools Will You Use as You Lead?

*The secret of getting ahead
is getting started.*
Mark Twain

Despite all the innovation in the virtual meeting space, one thing has not changed since the first conference call back in 1915: the audio environment is still the most important element in any virtual meeting. Our Six Principle Model is the only model that directly addresses how to be an effective leader in an all auditory environment. As we have illustrated in previous chapters, even when you're using video conferencing or avatar-based platforms, what happens on the audio determines the success or failure of your meeting. The question you must answer now is where to begin?

Two Simple Steps to Take Before Your Next Virtual Meeting

The first step in developing your unique leadership style is to review Chapter 2 and select the one principle which resonates with you most. Experiment with applying that principle during your next virtual meeting or class. After the meeting, ask yourself the following questions:

- What worked as I applied this principle?

- What challenges did I have using this principle during my meeting?

- What could I have done better?

- Based upon how my participants responded, what would I do differently next time?

Once you have mastered one principle, begin working on the next one.

The second step is turn to Appendix A and decide which items on the "Guidelines for Participants" (Attendees/Students) are applicable to the type of virtual meeting you will be leading. Once you have identified those items, create your customized "Guidelines for Participants" to fit your leadership style and the type of meeting you will be leading. Keep this list as short and simple as possible.

Always distribute the guidelines prior to your meeting/class. Review the key elements at the beginning of your meeting. If someone new is joining an on-going meeting, make sure they receive a copy as well. Byron recommends personally explaining the guidelines as a way to make the new person feel they are part of the group.

Stay Focused on Your Participants: Use "You," Not "I" or "Me"

The most important lesson I learned from Byron when I was first learning to lead teleclasses was to focus on the people on the call, not on my content or delivery. His advice was,

When you have a strong connection with your participants, they will forgive almost any mistake you make.

This applies to all types of virtual meetings and face-to-face meetings as well. The content and the slides are not as important as your connection with your participants.

As mentioned earlier, a simple way to be more participant-focused is to use "you" language as opposed to using "I" or "me." Even if you're delivering a keynote based upon your personal story, top speakers always pivot back to what will empower or inspire their audiences. This comes back to Principle #1: "People listen for their reasons, not yours."

Putting "you" to work

Did you know using "you" is not only a powerful tool in your virtual meetings, but in articles, social media, and blog posts as well? The following content template is the one I use for my articles on *Inman*

News. It also works equally well for virtual meetings. This approach integrates using "you" language with Principle #2, "People support what they help to create."

- Always start with a hook asking the reader or your participants to answer a question about themselves or by describing a specific benefit they will receive from reading/listening to what you have to say. (The first sentence in the previous paragraph uses a "hook.")

- Discuss your key points. This can be quoting experts, sharing a story or video, explaining what has worked for others, etc. Make it as fun and engaging as possible.

- If you share a personal story, always tie it back to how it applies to your readers/audience. In other words, move as quickly as possible from "I" back to "you."

- Share specific steps each person can take to implement what you have covered.

- Conclude with takeaways, suggested action steps for your participants/readers, or the results they can hope to achieve if they implement what they just heard or read.

While using "you" in one-on-one conversations can be accusatory and can diminish your connection, using "you" when leading virtual meetings rather than "I" or "me," is one of the quickest ways to strengthen your connection with your participants. Take advantage of it.

Case Study:
Twelve Real World Applications
of The Six Principle Model

Once you master The Six Principle Model for leading auditory meetings, you will find it provides a powerful foundation for any other type of virtual or face-to-face meeting you may lead. Would you like more examples of how you can apply The Six Principle Model in your company or organization? Here are 12 examples from our virtual meetings.

Audio-Only Meetings

1. **Conference calls**

   Millions of conference calls take place daily in virtually every type of organization and business. "Monday Morning Blues" from Chapter 3 illustrates what a poorly led conference call is like. Simple strategies such as starting on time, controlling the background noise on the call and having participants say their names first when they speak, will go a long way towards making any conference calls you lead more effective.

   Verticals we have worked with using The Six Principles to improve the quality of their conference calls include education, insurance, medical, non-profits, project managers, real estate, plus state and local governments.

2. **Teleclasses (training by phone)**

   Byron and I have been leading teleclasses since 1997. The following simple model provides a framework you can use with almost any teleclass you lead. It works equally well for training held on synchronous video platforms as well.

   - Prepare a list of 10-15 questions addressing the key content you plan to cover.

   - Once you have reviewed the key meeting guidelines ("Say your name first," "pause," etc.) open your teleclass by asking about the topics the group would most like to cover. You could also ask about a challenge they're currently facing as it relates to the topic of your class or meeting.

   - Help participants be more concise by asking them to limit their comments to no more than two sentences. If someone goes over, gently remind them of the two-sentence challenge.

- Track shares using a spreadsheet (and attendance if required). If your group has 15 or fewer participants, it's smart to hear from everyone at the beginning and the end of the call. Otherwise take up to 5-10 shares. Keep in mind somewhere between 30-50 percent of the group will have the same or similar challenges.

- Discuss the most important items to the group in rank order. (Principle #1, People listen for their reasons, not yours" and Principle #2, People support what they help to create.) This allows you to cover what matters most first.

- Take notes during your meeting to capture challenges, solutions, and other takeaways.

- FreeConferenceCall.com is the most popular conference calling solution internationally. You can also use the audio-only features on Zoom, Skype, or Google Hangouts. Each of these platforms allows you to record the call. You can obtain a written transcript of your meeting by loading your recording into Otter.ai. You can also record directly into Otter as well.

- Always let participants know they have the right to pass on commenting during your teleclass. Forcing someone to comment against their will breaks your connection, although nudging them by asking, "I want to hear from everyone," usually works.

- To wrap up your teleclass, ask everyone for a one-sentence takeaway or one action step they will be taking from being on the call. Byron usually ends his teleclasses and group coaching calls with a simple command:

    One word! Name first! What did you get from today? Go!

    This approach eliminates long shares at the end of the call and helps you to end on time.

- After the teleclass, share your meeting notes plus any additional information not covered during the meeting.

3. **One-on-one coaching, group coaching, and mastermind groups**
   We conduct all our one-on-one coaching and group coaching calls by phone. Telephone-based coaching has the additional advantage of allowing the client to attend their coaching session from almost anywhere. This is a major benefit for busy clients who spend a lot of time on the road.

   We also do all our group coaching calls by phone. These calls may be in addition to the live training we conduct via video conferencing or webinar, or as a supplement to the courses we offer through the Digital Chalk Learning Management System. Over the years, we have also used telephone-based mastermind groups for a wide variety of purposes, including creating training content, soliciting expert advice on projects we are undertaking, business consulting, etc.

   Occasionally we will have one-on-one clients or group coaching clients who would like to hold their coaching sessions face-to-face meeting on Skype or Zoom. Once they experience how much more they can accomplish and how comfortable they feel on a telephone-based coaching call, they always opt for coaching over the phone.

   There are three reasons this is the case. First, when you talk on the phone with the receiver next to your ear or with a headset, you are in intimate space, not professional space. This boosts connection and trust. Second, the visuals are distracting. Third, it's easier to work on tough problems when you don't have to worry about how you look on screen.

4. **Panel preparation for conferences and virtual meetings**
   One of the secrets to moderating a great panel is to conduct a panel prep (pre-meeting) by phone. From this meeting, you generate the questions you will ask your panelists on stage. I started using this approach back in 2007 with my first Awesome Females in Real Estate Conference and still use it today for any panel I moderate.

I also like to create a timeline for participants so they know how much time they will have for each question. For example, if we're doing a 20-minute panel with three panelists, each panelist will have about six minutes each to answer 3-4 questions. This translates into one-two minutes per question. This approach allows them to practice their responses on the call. The result is they feel more comfortable on stage and most give more concise answers to the questions as well. If someone does become long-winded on stage, "Pause" works beautifully in this scenario as well.

5. **Making your meetings and conferences as relevant as possible**
Each year I meet by phone with past conference attendees to identify high interest topics for our next conference. (Principle #2, "People support what they help to create," and Principle #4, "Surface the wisdom of the group.") This keeps the conference fresh, focused on what matters most to the women who attend, as well as building "Connection, connection, connection" (Principle #3) prior to the actual event.

6. **Virtual Book Club**
In the face of the pandemic, book clubs have been flourishing on video conferencing platforms. Over the years, I have hosted several book clubs as a teleclass. A well-run teleclass provides a greater degree of safety and intimacy than video-based meetings. It also allows more people to express their opinions minus any judgmental looks another participant may have. Again, the safety of the group is something every leader must fiercely protect. Once you lose the sense of safety and trust, it's hard to get it back.

Video Conferencing

7. **Live online classes and webinars**
The COVID-19 pandemic resulted in the mass migration of meetings to video meeting platforms. The result has been a blurring of what constitutes an online class vs. a webinar. Perhaps

the simplest way to distinguish the two is whether you conduct your meeting with the participant video feed turned on or off. For example, when I lead online CE classes for Texas Realtors, all participants are visible and can interact with me live any time during the meeting.

In contrast, many of my corporate clients continue to use GoToMeeting, GoToWebinar, and Webex delivery platforms where only the moderator and panelists video feeds are visible, and interaction takes place using the chat and via polling.

8. **Pre-recorded classes for learning management systems**

As discussed in Chapter 11, trainers can record training sessions directly on to their computer or use one of the cloud recording apps such as Camtasia, Adobe Premiere, or Final Cut Pro. They also have the option to record on Zoom, Skype, and Microsoft Teams, or directly into the LMS as well.

No matter what platform you use, remember to record the meeting in both in MP4 (video) and MP3 (audio-only) which makes editing the video easier as well as allowing you to repurpose the audio for podcasts or other purposes.

9. **Virtual conferences**

Due to COVID-19, we had to shift our 14th Annual Awesome Females in Real Estate Conference to a virtual format. After watching the issues during other virtual conferences where the meeting planners tried to conduct their entire conference live, we decided to pre-record 28 of our 34 sessions and replay them back at the scheduled time for the conference. For the six live sessions including our charitable auction and meet-and-greet session, we used Zoom and displayed all participants using "gallery view."

Our decision turned out to be a homerun. We had one minor glitch with the delivery where we had to shift the replay from my GM's computer to my computer, but the sessions were all delivered on time and came off without a glitch.

As noted in Chapter 6, virtual conference attendees become frustrated when they are unable to share resources and comments during the session. Moreover, even when participants were unable to attend the event live, they still want the chat to be visible in the replay. Based upon this feedback, we asked all our speakers and panelists to join the chat during their session.

The chat for the pre-recorded sessions was on fire with comments, questions bouncing back and forth between the speakers and the audience, shared links, and other resources. The chat also enabled participants to connect with the speakers in real time and to follow up with them after the conference. The six live sessions strengthened connections within the group while also allowing us to raise over $10,000 for breast cancer research.

While I hope we will be able to have our next conference in person, if we do need to go virtual, we plan on using exactly the same approach as we used this time.

10. **Video meetings for screen-sharing and product demonstrations**

    For many years we used Join.me to do screen sharing, whether it was to collaborate on our training, work on our website, or to conduct a product demonstration. In 2017 we shifted to Zoom. Both platforms provided a simple way to preview our products for potential customers and to answer their questions on the fly. This goes to Principles #1 and #2, "People listen for their reasons, not yours," and "People support what they help to create."

11. **Video conferencing platforms for recording interviews, podcasts, radio shows, and YouTube videos**

    We first launched RealEstateCoach Radio in 2010. Until 2017, we did all our guest mentor interviews using the recording feature on our teleconference lines. In late 2017, we moved to Zoom for recording both our audio and video podcasts.

    In mid-2020, I began linking my *Inman News* column to our RealEstateCoach Uncensored podcast that I co-host with Greg McDaniel. Great written content coupled with a strong video has proven to be a powerful combination resulting in us consistently placing in the top 5 contributed articles every week.

12. Hybrid meetings: In-person coupled with video-conferencing
Just before we went to press, I had a chance to lead my first hybrid meeting with a group of live attendees along with participants joining remotely on Zoom. The meeting set up was unusual in that we had two large conference tables. I was seated in the center with the masked attendees sitting at least eight feet away from me on the other side of the two tables. My laptop was on the conference table to my left. My PowerPoint slides, the video feed from the live group, plus the video feeds from remote attendees on Zoom were displayed on a large screen at the head of the table to my left.

While I always use The Six Principle Model to build engagement, my focus was almost exclusively on the live attendees. Granted, the company's technology director was handling Zoom and monitoring the chat, but I don't recall any questions or comments coming from the virtual participants.

An additional challenge was that when I looked to my right, the Zoom audience only saw the back of my head. I noticed the situation immediately, but there was no way to correct it given the limitations of the room setup.

As we have said repeatedly throughout this book, every session you lead is a chance for you to grow your leadership skills. The in-person engagement was high, and the post session feedback was great. Nevertheless, I could have done a better job of engaging our virtual attendees. Remember, acknowledge what you do right, but also ask what you could have done better. That's the best way to continue to grow your leadership skills.

Where to Concentrate Your Focus

As you finish this book and embark on your personal leadership journey, here are our top recommendations about where to concentrate your efforts.

Byron's Top 10 Recommendations:

1. **Avoid making your meetings unnecessarily difficult**
   The more you focus on yourself, your content, and your delivery, the harder it will be for you to lead the group.

2. **Focus on your strengths**
   As you tell the story of your leadership journey, remember to focus on what you did well rather than on your weaknesses and what went wrong. Every leader makes mistakes no matter how competent they are. Learn from your mistakes and continue expanding your repertoire of what you do well.

3. **Avoid wasting time rationalizing what went wrong**
   Instead, identify various options you could have used, select an option, and then apply it the next time you encounter a similar situation. For example, if people are talking over each other on an audio-only meeting, asking them to say their name first reduces the problem dramatically.

4. **Never underestimate the importance of Principle #6, "What you do is what you get"**
   If you attempt to control others, criticize a participant in front of the group, become angry, rude, or impatient, your participants will model what you do. Eventually the behavior you modeled will be directed back at you.

5. **Constantly work to upgrade your skills**
   Whether it's applying The Six Principle Model, your slides, delivery, handouts, etc., there are two important questions to ask after every meeting:

   What went right?

   What steps can I take on my next meeting to improve?

   Remember, small, consistent steps taken over time produce major results.

6. **Be okay with saying, "I don't know"**
   One of the smartest phrases any leader can learn to say is, "I don't know" and to follow up by asking the group for their feedback. Even when you think you do know, be curious and bounce the question back to the group. For example,

   > *John just raised an interesting question about the timing of this initiative. I'd like to ask the group, "What's your take on this situation?"*

7. **Avoid letting success go to your head**
   Sometimes success will go to a leader's head. When that happens, the leader has shifted to being me-focused rather than being participant-focused. This is a step backwards rather than forward because it breaks the connection. If you find yourself being more focused on how good you are as opposed to being participant focused, pivot back to The Six Principles and focus there instead.

8. **When you decide to emulate a role model, stay true to yourself**
   When you decide to emulate a role model, always do it in a way that is authentic to you. For example, if you want to inject more humor into your sessions and you're not very good at being funny, search for funny pictures or short videos that make people laugh. It's a simple solution that achieves the same result—you made your participants laugh.

9. **There is no one right path to effective leadership**
   The path you will take is unique to you and your personal strengths. Learn from others, from your mistakes, and from always searching for ways to be better. Constant improvement over time is the name of the game.

10. **When the magic happens**
    Finally, there will be a moment when you realize you have led a really great virtual meeting. You can feel it during the meeting and so will your participants. You can't try to make it happen—it just happens, and you'll know it. While your participants will

give you accolades, what matters most is knowing you delivered an extraordinary virtual meeting that created the results you set out to achieve. Always remember, learning is a continuous process—the more you learn, the better you will be.

Bernice's Top 10 Recommendations:

1. **Prioritize**
   When you purchased this book, what did you hope to learn? What problems did you hope to solve? As we mentioned at the beginning of the book, the strategies and tactics are not the issue—it's how you show up as a leader. We urge you to apply The Six Principles to your personal priorities first because it will make solving any issues you encounter easier to handle. Remember, if you have a strong connection with your participants, they will overlook almost any mistake you make.

2. **Start using "you" language now**
   No matter what type of meeting you are leading, using "you" language rather than "I" or "me" language is a practical step you can take today to start leading more effective virtual meetings tomorrow. This simple shift also allows you to tackle three of The Six Principles simultaneously: Principle #1, "People listen for their reasons, not yours;" Principle #2, "Surface the wisdom of the group;" and Principle #3, "Connection, connection, connection." Because of the powerful influence this simple shift has on your connection with your participants, the sooner you implement this step the better.

3. **People are hungry to be heard**
   Even if you never plan on holding a talking circle, read the guidelines for conducting a Talking Circle in Appendix B. Byron and I have used talking circles across multiple verticals both in the private and public sector for over two decades. Everyone is hungry to be heard and to feel what they say matters. Listening and being able to acknowledge your participants for their contributions is an important part of

making the magic of connection happen. It's also a powerful tool for generating solutions to challenging problems as well.

4. **Never make a participant wrong, especially in front of the group**
   Whenever you criticize a participant, make a participant wrong, or make a joke at a participant's expense, you not only break the connection and destroy the trust in your meeting, you shut down future discussion and participation as well.

5. **The power of "pause"**
   I use the word "pause" regularly, whether it's when a participant is having a technology problem, a guest on my radio show or YouTube channel has veered off topic, or a panelist is running over their allotted time. For example, if Susan is off on a tangent, interrupt her by saying,

   Susan, would you please pause for a moment?

   Assuming she has said at least one thing that is tied to the topic, follow up by saying,

   I want to circle back to something you just said that was important.

   At this point you would briefly mention what she said, thank her for sharing her perspective, and invite others to comment. Alternatively, you could shift gears and move on to another topic.

6. **Pray for sunshine, be prepared for rain**
   No piece of technology functions perfectly 100 percent of the time. Bandwidth issues are pervasive, participants joining from their cell phones consistently experience dropped calls, and even the most stable internet connection can become unstable. Consequently, you must always be prepared to lead an audio-only meeting.
   This is where Principle #5, "Flex your flexibility muscle," really matters. Being able to lead using only the auditory feed of

your meeting (coupled with a handout if needed) is a skill you will use for many years to come.

7. **Simplify and systematize**

    We have provided you with a number of resources and strategies to systematize the process of leading virtual meetings. The first step is simplifying wherever possible and then creating systems to address as many of the elements in your virtual meeting as possible.

    To do this, review the various strategies, mistakes to avoid, and other supporting materials provided in this book. Next, decide which ones you want to use as you lead your virtual meetings or classes.

    For example, edit the Guidelines for Participants so it fits how you lead. Next, decide when and how you will make it available to your participants, whether it's via email before the meeting or in the chat when you first launch the meeting.

    Once you make these decisions, you can create a system you can follow every time you lead a virtual meeting. The more systems you implement, the less effort leading an effective meeting will require.

8. **Your self-care has a powerful impact on your ability to lead**

    Make it a point to get plenty of sleep the night before any meeting you lead. If you're leading in the morning, always have a nourishing meal—coffee alone can spike your blood sugar levels making you edgy and less able to cope with any challenges that may occur. Failure to engage in adequate self-care will also make handling technology and the other challenges you encounter more difficult.

    Again, Zoom fatigue is real. If at all possible, limit the number of Zoom meetings you lead to two or three days per week. Conduct your other meetings by phone whenever possible. Your energy level will be better, you won't have to waste time preparing to do a video meeting, and you have the freedom to conduct your meeting wherever you choose—win-win-win.

9. **When something goes wrong, here's how to keep your cool**
   If you are rested and well-prepared, it's much easier to stay calm when crazy things happen. Anticipate what can go wrong as best you can (technology issues, getting bumped off the meeting while you're leading, disruptive or long-winded participants, etc.) and create your personal "Plan B" on what you will do if that issue occurs.

   In the case where you make a major mistake, address the issue head-on. I find the words, "I goofed," are an easy way to own you were responsible for the mistake. Also, as Byron has pounded into my brain for over two decades, avoid rationalizing or explaining. Most people don't care what the reason was for your mistake and your explanation may only make matters worse. Own the mistake and move on.

10. **Keep taking baby steps**
    Please heed this warning. Trying to do too much at once will overwhelm you. Identify one aspect of leading that you would like to work on during your next virtual meeting. Once you master that item, move on to the next one. Again, small steps taken over time lead to extraordinary results.

How Will You Know When You Have Mastered The Six Principles?

The process of mastery comes from consistently seeking feedback and always working to upgrade your performance. As mentioned repeatedly, the process of applying The Six Principles begins by observing what works vs. what doesn't work. The only barometer that matters is how effective you are with the people you are leading.

As you begin working with a principle, determine whether your participants are more engaged or less engaged. Then, simply do more of what works and less of what doesn't work. Be willing to try new things and experiment.

The leaders who learn the fastest do so when they honor all parts of their path—the successes, the mistakes, and the failures. Keep your focus on your participants and you'll quickly learn what does and does not work for them.

Choice is an essential part of mastery. There will be times you will be leading a virtual meeting and a participant will attempt to undermine what you hope to achieve. Even in these situations, The Six Principles provide a powerful tool allowing you to quickly work through the situation while also maintaining collaboration and creativity to the greatest extent possible. The key is to trust using this process regardless of how many mistakes and brick walls you may encounter.

Chapter 12 Key Points

1. The Six Principles are your road map charting your unique path to virtual meeting success.

2. Review The Six Principles in Chapter 2 to determine which one resonates with you most. Begin working with that principle on your next virtual meeting. Once you feel comfortable with your first choice, go to the second choice and work on implementing it.

3. Customize the "Guidelines for Participants" for the types of virtual meetings you lead. Always distribute them prior to the first meeting or class.

4. Use "You" language rather than "I" or "me" to stay focused on participants.

5. Review the Real-World Applications of The Six Principle Model plus our respective Top 10 Recommendations. Identify at least three you will begin working to implement in your virtual meetings.

As Lao Tzu once said:
A journey of one thousand miles begins with a single step.

What will be your first step?

Finally, Byron and I would like to express our heartfelt gratitude to you for buying our book. Always remember you are a unique leader. Smile, stay focused on learning, and laugh often. Mastery is closer than you ever imagined!

Acknowledgements

First and foremost, we would like to express our deepest appreciation to our fantastic team at RealEstateCoach.com and BrokerageUP! Inc. who contributed to the creation of this book:

Shane Bowlin who was the unrelenting force responsible for LGVM becoming a reality. She began lobbying me back in 2019 to update our 2011 book *No More Lame Conference Calls*. With the advent of the COVID-19 pandemic, it became increasingly apparent millions of leaders could benefit from our experience leading virtual meetings using The Six Principle Model. As with each of my six previous books, Shane has guided this process from start to finish including editing, laying out the final manuscript, proofing, locating our graphics designers, overseeing the work with our publisher, coordinating the website design, marketing, and a host of other tasks too numerous to list.

Miriam Valere for her outstanding work creating our training collateral and for her meticulous editing.

D. Todd Ferrell who has cleaned up more issues on our videos and training than I care to count.

Rebecca Finkel for her wonderful cover design for this book.

Although she is no longer with us, my dear friend and mentor of over 30 years Marilyn Naylor. Marilyn did extensive work with the Native American community. She first introduced me to the Native American talking circle in the 1990s. My 2007 book *Going Where* was based upon her work. I personally believe the Talking Circle is the most powerful collaboration tool any leader can use today.

We would also like to acknowledge the following:

Annette Anthony, Deborah Falcone, and Dena Jones for sharing how their respective companies have used Zoom to successfully maintain and grow their businesses during the pandemic.

Leslie Appleton Young, Sara Sutachan, and Debra Trappen for their pioneering work on the California Association of Realtors WomanUP! Initiative. I was honored to be involved in the research, interview 75 of the top female leaders in real estate using Zoom, and write three different white papers sharing our results. Their decision to deliver their 2020 conference using Virbela created a pretty steep learning curve for me which turned out to be a great addition to this book.

Teresa Boardman, fellow columnist at *Inman News,* for her article on "How to Create a Zoom Room."

The late Jon Douglas whose advice back in 1994 has been a guiding principle in my business ever since. After a competitor ripped off the training I had spent a year creating and I was practically in tears, he told me:

> *Bernice, there will always be copycats who try to rip us off. All we have to do is to be six months ahead of the competition and we will dominate the market.*

The advice is as true today as it was back then.

Deb Hernandez who pioneered the use of Zoom to deliver Continuing Education classes back in 2012. Deb hired me to lead my first Zoom CE classes in 2015. When the pandemic hit, her visionary work allowed the Texas Realtors to quickly pivot to using Zoom for association business as well as professional development classes.

Brad Inman, Publisher of *Inman News* (Inman.com), for publishing my weekly real estate advice columns since 2001. I am especially grateful to the Inman community of readers, leaders, and innovators who have supported me for so many years. A special shoutout to Senior Editor Dani Vanderboegh whose journalistic integrity is a role model for the entire publishing industry and who constantly challenges me to grow my writing skills.

Ted Laatz, Vice President of Events and Affiliated Services for Virbela, who gave me a personal tour of the Virbela campus along with "a boat ride around the island."

Michael Lissack for the object lesson in "looking straight at the camera."

Greg McDaniel, my broadcast partner at RealEstateCoach Uncensored on YouTube, who has "never met a camera or microphone he doesn't like" and who can go toe-to-toe with me when it comes to spinning "spaghetti" on our broadcasts.

The late Lou Piatt who gave me the seemingly impossible task of delivering training to 60 offices with no budget—I would never have met Byron, Thomas Leonard, or experienced a teleclass.

Kevin Turner who launched my audio podcast career back in 2011 and motivated me back in 2017 to make the move to video podcasting.

Acknowledgements

A special thanks to the many contributions of all the leaders, participants, students, and clients who have helped us "Surface the wisdom of the group" for the 25 plus years we have been leading virtual meetings.

Finally, to our family members for a lifetime of love and support. I'm certain they're astounded someone would pay for a book we wrote about "talking on the phone."

Appendix A:
Guidelines for Participants

Review the list of "Guidelines for Participants" and identify which ones apply best to the type of virtual meeting you will be leading. Make sure your participants receive your meeting guidelines prior to the meeting. Here's what to include:

For both audio-only and interactive video conferencing include the following:

1. How to log into the meeting.

2. The phone numbers to call if they're joining the meeting by phone and whom to contact if they have trouble logging on to the meeting.

3. How to mute their audio based upon the platform they are using or by using the mute function on their phone.

4. Silence your mobile devices. If you have a landline, turn the ringer off. This will avoid interruptions from incoming calls.

5. If you have beeps or other sounds to notify you of incoming email, social media notifications, or texts, turn those off on both your computer plus any other mobile devices.

6. For audio-only meetings video conferencing where the participant's name is not displayed, always remind them to, "Say your name first."

For video conferencing meetings:

1. Check your camera prior to the meeting to make sure it is at eye level.

2. Sit in a well-lit location. Avoid sitting in any area that is poorly lit, where there is a bright light source that washes out part of the video feed, or with a window directly in back of you.

3. Make sure your name is visible on your video feed as well as the names of all the participants. (This is generally an option either in the general or video settings.)

4. To minimize bandwidth issues, close all applications on your computer and other devices with the exception of your meeting platform.

5. If you decide to use global mute when participants log on but still keep their video feed, advise participants their video will be active, but their audio will be muted when they join. This is especially important for large meetings where background noise is a major issue.

6. If you're using global mute, use the "hand-raise" feature to call on those who want to speak. This avoids having people talk over each other.

7. If you are not using global mute because you have a small meeting, it's still smart to ask participants to mute themselves in case there is an incoming phone call or other interruption that could disturb other participants. The challenge with this approach, however, is participants often start to speak and fail to realize they are still on mute.

8. If you have participants who are unfamiliar with the platform you are using, record a brief video explaining how to use the features you will employ during your meeting. Alternatively, have a second host or moderator available to assist participants in real time.

Appendix B:
Guidelines for Creating a Talking Circle

The Talking Circle is an ancient tool that helps people today face 21st Century challenges. While psychologists have been conducting group therapy since 1940, Native Americans have used the Talking Circle to process difficult situations for centuries. Today's support groups, teleclasses, group coaching, group therapy, and virtual meetings are offshoots of this ancient technique practiced for centuries by indigenous people across the world.

In many Western cultures, talking is a competitive sport. We interrupt each other constantly and compete to make ourselves heard. As a result, many of us have poor listening skills coupled with a strong need to be heard. Poor listening skills translate into poorer relationships and consistent miscommunication.

In contrast, Native American culture values cooperation over competition. This is reflected in virtually every aspect of their lives and lifestyles. Native Americans engage in conversation quite differently from the American competitive style: they listen, usually looking down. They do not establish eye contact until the person speaking is completely finished. When they speak, they fully expect to be able to completely finish their thought without interruption or before the conversation goes off to another person.

The Talking Circle fully expresses this style of conversation. In Native American culture, a talking stick is passed around the circle in a clockwise direction. Talking Circles can range in size from two people to groups of 300 or more.

During a Talking Circle, no voice is right, wrong, overemphasized, or disregarded. When engaged to its fullest potential, the Talking Circle transcends individual egos, exclusive dichotomies (e.g., us versus them), and fragmented, disconnected outcomes. It gives voice to all participants, not only to a vocal few.

Talking Circle Guidelines for Your Participants

The Talking Circle is flexible enough to accommodate the needs of almost any group while also providing a structure that produces positive outcomes. Nevertheless, guidelines about how to listen and participate in a talking circle are a must, no matter what type of group it is. Without clear guidelines, trust and communication disintegrate. This in turn could result in the situation the circle seeks to address becoming worse rather than better.

Here are the talking circle guidelines I distributed to my students at the beginning of each semester. When I have led talking circles live, I review these guidelines orally prior to beginning the circle.

1. The person holding the talking stick is the only one with the right to speak, even if he or she takes a long time to think about what to say and there is a pause in the conversation. If the circle members do not know each other, they may begin the circle by introducing themselves.

2. Listen attentively. The only time you may speak is when you are holding the talking stick.

3. When the talking stick comes to you, share your thoughts on the topic. Be concise. You may also share "whatever is in your heart." In other words, even though there is a topic, the conversation is by no means limited to a single topic. You are free to say whatever you are experiencing, without limitation, and in the safe and comfortable knowledge that nobody will criticize or interrupt you.

4. Do not comment on what anyone else says. You are only to comment on your experience, not on anyone else's experience. Share your personal perspective without passing judgment on anything said by other members of your circle. Keep your body language still. No negative comments or critical statements are allowed. Furthermore, each person must wait his or her turn to speak.

5. In Native American culture, especially if there is a large group, when a person speaks too long, people around the circle begin to cough discreetly. "Too long" is subjective. Most people speak for a few minutes although this is contingent upon the size of the group, the topic, and how long the group wants to spend together. If you have the talking stick and notice that others are coughing, it's time to pass

it along. (Use of a timer is considered to be inappropriate because it interrupts that natural flow of the conversation.)

6. Everyone in the circle speaks. The talking stick is passed to all members of the circle until everyone feels they have expressed what they wanted to say. It is acceptable to pass the talking stick without speaking, although everyone is encouraged to say what is in his or her heart. In most circles, members have pretty much had their say once the talking stick has been passed around two or three times.

7. In Native American culture, the circle traditionally ends with a prayer, however, it can end with each person saying thank you and passing the talking stick to the center of the circle.

Outcomes You Can Achieve Using the Talking Circle

Whether you use the Talking Circle in a business, educational, or personal setting here are the types of outcomes you can hope to achieve:

1. Improved listening skills including listening without judgment.

2. Increased trust and intimacy.

3. Resolution of family and business disputes in a way that promotes communication and trust.

4. By allowing every participant to speak and express their feelings in a non-judgmental environment, the Talking Circle helps to build trust among the participants. In a work setting, this means reaching goals more quickly. It also results in more cohesive teams because trust levels are high.

5. Talking Circles also work well in family environments. Each family member can have their say without interruption. This serves to lessen conflicts because each person can share his or her perspective.

Using the Talking Circle as a Counseling Tool

For coaches, psychologists, and similar professions, the circle has the following benefits:

1. **Active listening**
   More than any other competency, the Talking Circle builds active listening. Since the counselor/coach is not required to comment or make recommendations on what others are saying, they can concentrate more fully on the client's concerns, goals, values, and beliefs. When Talking Circles are held face-to-face (rather by phone or on-line), this approach strengthens their ability to interpret words, tone of voice, and body language. The Talking Circle experience normally heightens awareness and increases focus. The Talking Circle is also a safe place where the client can vent or clear difficult situations without judgment or attachment on the counselor/coach's part.

2. **Powerful questioning**
   To ask powerful questions, you must be an active, attentive listener. The Talking Circle creates an environment of non-attachment. According to Tony Alexis of the Nakota Sioux Nation, this allows the leader of the circle to "sit on the rock upon which the other person sits and to see the world from the rock where the other person sits." When there is no judgment, there is no need for the individual who is speaking to justify their choices. Instead, the leader is better able to open the space so that the client can take positive steps to move forward.

3. **Creating awareness**
   When we speak, we shift our focus from the client to what we want to say. Often times we are formulating suggestions even before the client finishes speaking. When the participants in a Talking Circle can speak without any interruption or verbal feedback from the counselor/coach, they become more attuned to their own inner wisdom and can more easily follow their own inner voice. When the client decides what actions to take, the

client is more likely to complete the action that leads to forward movement.

4. **Insights from Talking Circle participants**

- *It was the first time in my life that I was respectfully heard without interruptions from friends and family. I felt free to share with no judgment. Our group had chemistry like people who had known each other for a long time.*

- *I learned how little mankind truly listens to another. Because we were given the freedom to say what was in our hearts, I learned more about my group members than I know about some of my friends. We all agreed this was a life-changing event.*

- *I tried the Talking Circle with my family and friends. I noticed that my friends and parents listen more than they did in the past. This event changed my life.*

About the Authors

Bernice L. Ross, Ph.D.

Bernice L. Ross, the CEO and President of BrokerageUP!, Inc. and RealEstateCoach.com, is an international author, speaker, and trainer. Bernice couples her expertise as a Professor Emeritus of Psychology with over 35 years of real estate sales and leadership experience. With over 1,200 published articles and four best-selling real estate books to her credit, *Inman News* called Bernice, "America's Top Real Estate Coach." Her research has documented the effectiveness of The Six Principle Model for conference calls, teleclasses, video-conferencing, webinars, and face-to-face meetings in both corporate and public sector environments.

Byron Van Arsdale, Co-Founder Lead Great Meetings and RealEstateCoach.com

Byron Van Arsdale, international speaker, Master Certified Coach, and presentation strategist, has worked with executives and professionals to lead exceptional face-to-face and virtual meetings since 1991. Thousands of virtual meeting leaders across Asia, Australia, Europe, North America, and New Zealand have used The Six Principle Model to increase meeting effectiveness and organizational productivity. He also served on the faculty of CoachU where he mentored over 2,000 new and experienced coaches using The Six Principle Model via teleclass.

Byron's coaching, training, and consulting clients include IBM, Kaiser Permanente, Oracle, Cisco, Charles Schwab, The Los Angeles Community College District, Motorola, City of Austin, Coldwell Banker, Koch Industries, The State of Texas, Kahala, and numerous other companies and public sector organizations. The Six Principle Model of Leadership is a proven method for leading and conducting effective virtual meetings within any organization.

CPSIA information can be obtained
at www.ICGtesting.com
Printed in the USA
BVHW090507270621
609933BV00002B/2